The Visual in Metaphysical Poetry

The Visual in Metaphysical Poetry

by

Mary Cole Sloane

Humanities Press
Atlantic Highlands, N. J.

First published in the United States of America in 1981 by Humanities Press Inc.
Atlantic Highlands, N.J. 07716

Library of Congress Cataloging in Publication Data

Sloane, Mary Cole.
  The visual in metaphysical poetry.

  Includes bibliographical references and index.
  1. English poetry—Early modern, 1500-1700—History and criticism. 2. Figures of speech. 3. Knowledge, Theory of. I. Title.
PR545.M4S57   821'.3'09   81-4193
ISBN 0-391-02299-7   AACR2

Manufactured in the United States of America

To Angeline Schumm Cole
and
to the memory of Matthew Fred Cole

Contents

Preface

When the writers of the Restoration and eighteenth century struggled to articulate their own theories of poetry, it was the metaphysical poetry of the immediate past which they singled out as embodying those characteristics most antithetical to their own underlying assumption that all art was the imitation of nature. And when Anthony Ashley Cooper, third Earl of Shaftesbury, needed an example to show precisely what good painting was not, he selected that example from the emblem tradition that had been so pervasive during the sixteenth and early seventeenth centuries. This was not mere coincidence. For between, for example, John Donne's "Holy Sonnets" and Alexander Pope's Virgilian eclogue, "Messiah," the epistemological emphasis had shifted away from innate ideas to ideas based on observation. Thus it was inevitable that the complexities of both the metaphysical conceit and the mind-teasing emblem would strike eighteenth-century critics as affectation.

Also inconsistent, although perhaps less so, with the far more objective classical emphasis of the eighteenth century was the meditative orientation that Louis L. Martz has shown to be so much a part of seventeenth-century poetry. Like the religious meditation, the emblem has been explored adequately in relation to metaphysical poetry. What has not been given sufficient emphasis is the impact that the interrelation of these two aspects of early seventeenth-century cultural interest, occurring during an epistemological revolution, had upon each other. The impact of the simultaneous existence of emblem, meditation, and epistemological upheaval had a profound effect on the visualizations one finds in metaphysical poetry. It accounts for much that is dissimilar, as well as similar, in the visual imagery of the metaphysical poets. Within metaphysical poetry itself, there is a progressive tendency away from the concept that knowledge is part of a universal system of analogies and toward an emphasis on knowledge gained directly from sensory experience.

Because I have limited my approach exclusively to the visual, I have tried to eliminate conclusions that would depend on textual explication of the poems. Also, I have not attempted to go deeply into the epistemological theories of John Locke, for he was after the fact as far as the metaphysical poets were concerned; and their own epistemological gropings are not discussed at length because, although crucial to the visual imagery in their poetry, they were at best tentative and inconclusive. I have dealt with emblems in the light of techniques they reveal rather than in relation to any influence that a given emblem might have had on a specific image.

I wish to express my appreciation to Professor John I. McCollum of the University of Miami for introducing me to the emblem literature; and I wish to thank those libraries that have either helped me find material or given me permission to use their resources. These are the British Library, the Folger Shakespeare Library, and the libraries of the University of Miami, the University of Florida, and Florida Atlantic University. I thank especially the Folger Shakespeare Library and the British Library for permission to reproduce emblem prints from their collections. I also wish to thank Oxford University Press for permission to quote from the poetry of John Donne, George Herbert, Henry Vaughan, Richard Crashaw, Thomas Traherne, and Sir John Davies; Houghton Mifflin Company for permission to quote *The Complete Poetical Works of Spenser,* Cambridge Edition, 1908; McGill-Queens University Press for permission to quote from Donne's *Devotions Upon Emergent Occasions;* and Princeton University Press for permission to quote from *The Hieroglyphics of Horapollo.*

Mary Cole Sloane

I

The Noblest Sense and the Book of Nature

Although we are aware of important differences among them, we customarily have placed five poets—John Donne, George Herbert, Henry Vaughan, Richard Crashaw, and Thomas Traherne—in one literary classification. Following Dryden's lead, we have applied a common term, "metaphysical," to their poetic output. The name has stuck despite a tendency to associate some of these poets with "mannerism," a category drawn from art history, and despite Louis L. Martz's perceptive suggestion that the common denominator in their poetry is the religious meditation. But, regardless of how we categorize them in broad and general terms, the five poets have eluded classification when it comes to the particulars of their poetic styles. This is especially true of definitions of the metaphysical conceit which, if tailored to fit the metaphors of Donne and Herbert, are somehow inappropriate when applied to the metaphors of Vaughan or Traherne.

What has only recently begun to be recognized is the impact on the metaphysical poets of the deep epistemological upheaval that occurred during the seventeenth century. Modern recognition of the significance of epistemology is becoming increasingly pertinent to our understanding of the intellectual milieu in which the metaphysical poets wrote.

Looking at metaphysical poetry in the light of how its creators felt they acquired knowledge raises the question of their relationship to the medieval concept of world order with which they, from the beginning of the twentieth century's revival of interest in them, often have been associated.[1] If the metaphysical poets were indeed

questioning accepted ways of knowing, it is unreasonable to
assume that they, either consciously or unconsciously, could leave
unchallenged the concept of a universe in which everything cor-
responded perfectly to everything else. It is even less reasonable to
assume that, writing after the Ptolemaic picture of world order had
received so many threatening blows, they could let that picture find
its way into their poetry unadulterated. There would, in this context, appear to be an inconsistency in the traditional appraisal of
the metaphysical poets' place in the history of thought. The inconsistency becomes overwhelmingly apparent if we concentrate our
attention on precisely how each of the metaphysical poets regarded
the visual world from which he obtained his metaphors.

To arouse our suspicions that metaphysical poetry was indeed
responsive to an epistemological upheaval, we need only compare
the attitude toward the senses of its first and last representatives,
Donne and Traherne. On Easter Sunday, 1628, John Donne told
the congregation that had gathered in the old Gothic Cathedral of
St. Paul's in London that "sight is so much the Noblest of all the
senses, as that it is all the senses."[2] His ultimate purpose in thus
elevating the sense of sight, as he explicated his Biblical text,[3] was
to debase it in order to impress upon the minds of his listeners that
man saw through a glass darkly. Earlier, reading from the book of
nature rather than the Book of scripture, he had noted that

Sight is the noblest sense of any one,
Yet sight hath only colour to feed on,
And colour is decai'd: summers robe growes
Duskie, and like an oft dyed garment showes.
                    (The first Anniversary, lines 353-356)[4]

Donne's wistful distrust of what he sees is a far cry from
Traherne's joyous exaltation later in the century in what his senses
enable him to experience:

For *Sight* inherits Beauty, *Hearing* Sounds,
        The *Nostril* Sweet Perfumes,
        All *Tastes* have hidden Rooms
Within the *Tongue;* and *Feeling Feeling* Wounds
    With Pleasure and Delight; but I
Forgot the rest, and was all Sight, or Ey.
    Unbodied and Devoid of Care,

Just as in Heavn the Holy Angels are.
   For Simple Sence
Is Lord of all Created Excellence.

             (The Preparative, lines 31-40)[5]

The juxtaposition of the two passages suggests that in regard to the validity of knowledge obtained through the senses a change has most certainly occurred. This could be expected, for the lives of the metaphysical poets spanned that period in intellectual history immediately preceding John Locke's refutation of the concept of the innate idea.

   The seventeenth century, writes K.G. Hamilton, saw the shift of the center of philosophical interest "from metaphysics to epistemology; from a concern with the nature and verbalization of truth to a primary interest in the way in which truth can become known."[6] The epistemological theories of the early church fathers and their heirs had been concerned basically with man's knowledge of God; how man came to know his immediate terrestrial environment was always subsidiary to that larger question. The philosophers who most influenced the mainstream of Medieval or Renaissance thought had not struggled with the sticky problem of sensory experience for it's own sake. Indeed, it would have been blasphemy to do so. Thus a certain measure of cautious skepticism had been almost mandatory, since it was precisely the search for knowledge that had been the original sin responsible for the fall of man and the consequent corruption not only of man, but also of the physical world itself. Man's presumption in the face of forbidden knowledge had brought upon him the wrath of God. Typically, the late sixteenth-century poet, Sir John Davies, asks in his philosophical verse-essay about the soul,

What is this *knowledge?* but the Skie-stolne fire,
  For which the *Thiefe* still chaind in Ice doth sit?
           (Nosce Teipsum, lines 41-42)[7]

   His Prometheus is accompanied by such other guilty human beings as Ixion, Phaeton, and Icarus. Approximately a half-century earlier, the emblematist Andreas Alciati had drawn examples from the same list for his *Emblematum Liber* of 1531. Sir Francis Bacon found it necessary, in *The Advancement of Learning,* published in 1605, to raise learning from the lowly position to which he felt it had fallen. His solution was one that frequently would be reverted to by men who found themselves in the guilt-producing dilemma between God and science. There *was* to Bacon a forbidden knowledge, a knowledge of God, that man could not arrive at through the use of his senses. But there also was a legitimate human knowledge—that of man's observable surroundings. It was, of course, this latter kind of knowledge that would be emphasized throughout the succeeding centuries.

When interest was moving during the Renaissance toward the latter kind of knowledge, those thinkers who were either directly or indirectly concerned had at their disposal two basic epistemological concepts which had been absorbed by the medieval philosophers into various theories concerning man's knowledge of God. From Plato had come the concept that everything that was available to the senses was in a state of flux and therefore could not present man with a knowledge of the real. Aristotle contributed the concept that the active intellect abstracted forms from images that existed materially in nature. Associated with Plato was the assumption that man was born with a faint memory of the ideal, while associated with Aristotle was the assumption that all knowledge was acquired through sensory experience. But the implications inherent in Aristotle's emphasis on the senses were not used to challenge the popular medieval concept of world order that persisted well into the Renaissance.

One need only to cite Donne's extensive use of microcosm-macrocosm imagery to illustrate that he, born in the early 1570's, must have absorbed the primarily Platonic belief in a universe made up of terrestrial-celestial correspondences—that emblematic concept of the universe that has been shown by E.M.W. Tillyard to be so much a part of Elizabethan poetry.[8] The seventeenth century would end, however, with an emphasis on the physical universe itself. This new emphasis was consistent with the materialism propounded by Thomas Hobbes in his *Leviathan* of 1651 and with the death-blow given to the Platonic concept of the innate idea by Locke when, in his *An Essay Concerning Humane Understanding* of 1691, he declared that the human mind at birth was a *tabula rasa*. Locke, in effect, provided a conscious epistemological rationale that could justify the Renaissance concept of art as the imitation of nature and that could provide the Augustan writers with a secure epistemological base on which to construct their various mimetic theories.[9] Placed thus between a period that emphasized the Platonic approach to epistemology and a period that followed a more Aristotelian approach, the metaphysical poets were in a unique position to respond to any suspicions concerning the old concept and also to consider any cultural glimmerings suggesting the new. Their predicament calls to mind a phrase that Roy Daniells used in regard to the metaphysical poets and the concept of mannerism. He wrote that with the concept available, the style of the metaphysical poets no longer seemed like an aberration "but rather as the logical development from Spenserian or Sidneyan smoothness and the necessary bridge from this island of stability to the Baroque *terra firma* on which the larger works of Milton are erected."[10] Because the metaphysical poets wrote on the eve of an epistemological revolution, it also might be possible to see their poetry as suggestive of a journey from the stable island of medieval epistemology to the *terra firma* of the *tabula rasa*. For in the seventeenth century it was quite possible for a poet seeking images to swing inconsistently back and forth between what were considered either primarily Aristotelian or primarily Platonic conceptions of knowledge obtained through the senses. The metaphysical poets seemed to have been uncommonly aware of this possibility; there is evidence that the epistemological problem surfaced with more directness than was really necessary for the creation of poetic imagery. They were, with the exception of Crashaw, highly suspicious of the concept of universal analogy. That this is so ultimately can be established through an analysis of their visual imagery. Although only Traherne consciously formulated an epistemological theory, the metaphoric challenge to the concept of universal analogy can be established at the outset. The new resolutions had not yet been articulated; but the old most certainly were found wanting.

That metaphoric challenge is evident in Donne's fondness for indiscriminately ransacking not only nature and art, but also diverse philosophic and scientific concepts for vehicles wherein to contain his wit.[11] One ransacking is most pertinent here, for it shows his attitude toward epistemology. In his *Ecclogue* of 1613, he playfully carried an aspect of medieval epistemology to the point of absurdity. His Idios, trying to explain to Allophanes why he was not at the court for the wedding of the Earl of Sommerset, argues that he did not need to be there because

> Kings (as their patterne, God) are liberall
> Not onely in fulnesse, but capacitie,
>   Enlarging narrow men, to feele and see,
> And comprehend the blessings they bestow.
>   So, reclus'd hermits often times do know
> More of heavens glory, then a worldling can.
>
> *(Ecclogue,* lines 44-49)

Idios, of course, is basing his argument on the assumption that man's mind is a microcosmic representation of the macrocosm:

> As man is of the world, the heart of man,
> Is an epitome of Gods great booke.
>
> *(Ibid.,* lines 51-52)

But Allophanes chides Idios for being so naively accepting:

> Dreamer, thou art.
> Think'st thou, fantastique that thou hast a part
> In the East-Indian fleet, because thou hast
>   A little spice, or Amber in thy taste?
>
> *(Ibid.,* lines 55-58)

Although the real reason behind Allophanes' challenge is that it gives him the opportunity to make laudatory statements about king and court, the challenge shows that Donne was aware of several epistemological possibilities and could subject to doubt, whether seriously or not, the generally accepted assumptions of his time.

The imagery used by Donne in the *Anniversary* poems is undoubtedly more seriously meant and thus more potentially significant than Allophanes' challenge of Idios' epistemology. When Donne wrote the poems to commemorate the death of the young Elizabeth Drury, he could not have anticipated the extent to which the problem of her identity would concern scholars in a more literal age. The "rich Soule which to her heaven is gone" has been variously identified. Therefore Frank Manley suggests that perhaps Elizabeth Drury as a symbol may be capable of too many associations to be pinned down to a single and specific one[12]. But Manley raises the possibility that the imagery is related to various

Renaissance concepts of wisdom,[13] and Hiram Haydn has interpreted the death of Elizabeth Drury as the repeal of natural law.[14] Both of these have epistemological implications, and an epistemological interpretation might indeed be valid. This is not to suggest, though, that other interpretations can be negated. But Donne's awareness of the epistemological upheaval of the seventeenth century is decidedly apparent when the *Anniversary* poems are compared to Sir John Davies' *Nosce Teipsum.*

While Donne presents us with a crumbling and disordered universe and Davies emphasizes harmony, neither challenges the assumptions that the fall of man clouded man's mind and that only death would bring man perfect knowledge. In *The second Anniversary,* which can be regarded as the fideistic answer to *The first Anniversary,*[15] Donne writes:

Thinke then, my soule, that death is but a Groome,
Which brings a Taper to the outward roome,
Whence thou spiest first a little glimmering light,
And after brings it nearer to thy sight:
For such approaches doth heaven make in death.

(lines 85-89)

Similarly, near the end of *Nosce Teipsum,* Davies warns his soul:

Know that thou canst know nothing perfectly,
While thou art Clouded with this flesh of mine.

(lines 1915-1916)

Like Donne, Davies could refer to human speculation as resulting in confusion:

One thinks the *Soule* is *Aire,* another Fire,
Another *Blood,* defus'd about the hart;
Another saith, the *Elements* conspire,
And to her *Essence* each doth give a part.

(Nosce Teipsum, lines 209-212)

But Davies sets out to resolve that confusion while Donne takes quite a different path:

Have not all soules thought
For many ages, that our body' is wrought

Of Ayre, and Fire, and other Elements?
And now they thinke of new ingredients,
And one Soule thinkes one, and another way
Another thinkes, and 'tis an even lay.

(The second Anniversary, lines 263-268)

Ultimately, Davies optimistically claims that

. . . in *mans minde* we finde an appetite
To *learne,* and *know the truth* of everie thing;
Which is connaturall, and borne with it
And from the *Essence* of the *Soule* doth spring.

(Nosce Teipsum, lines 1305-1308)

For Davies, with a security of which Donne would not have been
remotely capable, can write of man's appetite for learning:

With this *desire* she hath a native *might*
To finde out everie truth, if she had time,
Th' innumerable effectes to sort aright,
And by degrees, from cause to cause to clime.

(Ibid, lines 1309-1312)

Davies, answering the challenge of atheism that became crucial
toward the end of the sixteenth century, polished every possible
conceptual weapon with which his culture provided him in order to
defeat Christianity's adversaries. R.L. Colie has suggested that
whereas "Davies had asserted that it was possible for the soul to
know, and organized his theory of knowledge around the soul,
Donne denied the soul knowledge even of itself."[16] Accepting on
faith that the soul was immortal, Donne would not have presum-
ed, as Davies did, to set up arguments to prove his point. Instead,
he declares unqualifiedly that such knowledge is beyond man's
capacity:

Thou neither know'st, how thou first cam'st in,
Nor how thou took'st the the poyson of mans sinne.
Nor dost thou, (though thou know'st, that thou art so)
By what way thou art immortall, know.

(The second Anniversary, lines 257-260)

Against the whole *nosce teipsum* theme he could imply a most
devasting warning:

Thou art too narrow, wretch, to comprehend
Even thy selfe.

(Ibid., lines 261-262)

In contrast, Davies, accepting traditional faculty psychology,
claimed:

That *Powre* which gave my eyes, the world to view;
  To view my selfe enfus'd an *inward light;*
  Whereby my *Soule,* as by a Mirror true,
  Of her owne forme may take a perfect sight.

(Nosce Teipsum, lines 193-196)

Although Donne's negation of man's potentiality for self
knowledge can be interpreted as a witty argument in support of his
eventual fideistic resolution, it nevertheless also supports what
becomes an epistemological theme in the *Anniversary* poems.
Charles Monroe Coffin has shown that Donne successfully but
without commitment could select imagery from both the
Ptolemaic and Copernican theories of the universe.[17] In the *Anniversary* poems, Donne successfully draws from various aspects
of the epistemological theories available to him and appraises them
as useless.

He suggests his epistemological orientation very early in *The
first Anniversary* by mourning the disappearance of the Platonic
innate idea when he complains that "memory" as well as sense
(line 28) has been lost. In *The second Anniversary* (lines 291-292),
he claims that it is pedantic for man to depend on fantasy, that
faculty of the soul responsible in scholastic philosophy for mental
apprehension. Furthermore, his departed Elizabeth is presented as
one who "first tried indifferent desires/By vertue . . ." *(Ibid,* lines
75-76) in a prince and court metaphor that recalls Davies' description of the soul's "prince," who reigns over the passions *(Nosce
Teipsum,* lines 1209-1216). But Donne's most devastating
metaphor of the loss of man's mental capacity is his passage that
concerns not function, but quality:

But this were light, did our lesse volume hold
All the old Text; or had wee chang'd to gold
Their silver; or dispos'd into lesse glasse
Spirits of vertue, which then scatter'd was.
But 'tis not so; w'are not retir'd, but dampt;

And as our bodies, so our mindes are crampt:
'Tis shrinking, not close weaving that hath thus,
In minde, and body both bedwarfed us.

(The first Anniversary, lines 147-154)

Looking inward, then, Donne finds no security whatever in the traditional approaches to knowledge. For, as Colie has put it, Donne was quite aware that "a crooked mind cannot measure a crooked world; man's ways of knowing are as skewed as the world they seek to know."[18] That "crooked world" itself, whose dominating images of decay and ugliness have been traced by Victor Harris to similar images in sources propounding the theory that man's fall initiated the world's progressive physical deterioration,[19] complicates the epistemological problem and presents a related esthetic one. Davies not only had found the mind adequate for its terrestrial purposes, but also had found the earth of sufficient value to account for man's delight in the visual arts *(Nosce Teipsum,* lines 997-1000). Donne, on the other hand, uses his emphasis on the sense of sight to negate the world's visual potentialities for either knowledge or beauty by eliminating all possibility of Aristotelian abstraction. One could, from a world that was a wan ghost, an ugly monster, a dry cinder, or even a dead and rotten carcass, perhaps still arrive at some kind of ideal abstraction. But the Donne who mourns the loss of a Platonic standard when he calls Elizabeth's death the loss of "the best, the first originall/of all faire copies" *(The first Anniversary,* lines 227-228), also sums up the distorted visual remains of a once perfect world as "fragmentary Rubbidge" *(The second Anniversary,* line 82) and thus utterly worthless. Looking outward, the eyes do not encounter anything of value,

For the worlds beauty is decai'd, or gone,
Beauty, that's colour, and proportion.

(The first Anniversary, lines 249-250)

Thus, to Donne, the traditional ways whereby man has known are of little or no avail for either religious or esthetic purposes. And we can in this light regard, at least in part, the lines that conclude Donne's famous passage claiming that the "new Philosophy calls all in doubt":

Prince, Subject, Father, Sonne, are things forgot,
For every man alone thinkes he hath got
To be a Phoenix, and that then can bee
None of that kinde, of which he is, but hee.

(The first Anniversary, lines 215-218)

Haydn has suggested that the passage reflects Montaigne's emphasis on man as individual rather than as type.[20] Regarded in the light of the *Anniversary* poems' negative references to epistemology, Donne's would-be phoenix becomes, certainly, an individual who has suffered the loss of the means of arriving at universals by whatever method. Donne's skepticism regarding man's ability to know himself is balanced by his skepticism regarding man's potential knowledge of the universe. Both would affect metaphorical manifestations of the visual.

Whether he liked it or not, Donne became his own phoenix in regard to esthetics. The door of classicism, from whatever direction he approached it, was closed to him. The techniques and content of classicism were available, but he had to use those techniques and reorder that content without reference to classical guidelines. He concludes *The first Anniversary* by recalling the Renaissance concept that the work of art has something that could preserve the universal:

Verse hath a middle nature: heaven keepes Soules,
The Grave keepes bodies, Verse the Fame enroules.

(lines 473-474)

But he endorses this concept hesitantly:

Nor could incomprehensiblenesse deterre
Mee, from thus trying to emprison her,
Which when I saw that a strict grave could doe,
I saw not why verse might not do so too.

(Ibid., lines 469-472)

Elsewhere he could take issue altogether with the prevailing Renaissance belief that the way to deal with man's mortality was to immortalize him in art. Writing of his own verses, he says:

Mine are short-liv'd; the tincture of your name
Creates in them, but dissipates as fast,

New spirits: for, strong agents with the same
Force that doth warme and cherish, us doe wast;
Kept hot with strong extracts, no bodies last:

So, my verse built of your just praise, might want
Reason and likelihood, the firmest Base,
And made of miracle, now faith is scant,
Will vanish soone, and so possesse no place,
And you, and it, too much grace might disgrace.
(To the Countesse of Bedford. On New-yeares day, lines 16-25)

Donne saw not only the mind being deprived of its correspondence
to the macrocosm but also saw man's mind emptied of any endow-
ment that would enable him to perceive correspondences if they
had existed. Thus he was presented with esthetic problems similar
to those that Erwin Panofsky found had beset the mannerist
painters who earlier had veered away from the esthetic security of
the High Renaissance. That security, Panofsky writes, had been
challenged by the question of whether the beautiful was an actual
possibility; in their search for an answer the mannerist theorists,
because of their emphasis on the individual artistic personality,
became conscious of the gap between the subject or mind and object.[21] Donne, who used the phoenix in The first Anniversary to
pejoratively exemplify man's need to be a unique individual, also
was aware of that gap. He gives his reasons:

For fluid vertue cannot be look'd on,
Nor can endure a contemplation.
As bodies change, and as I do not weare
Those spirits, humors, blood I did last yeare,
And, as if on a streame I fixe mine eye,
That drop, which I looked on, is presently
Pusht with more waters from my sight, and gone,
So in this sea of vertues, can no one
Bee insisted on.[22]
(Obsequies to the Lord Harrington, brother to the Lady Lucy,
Countesse of Bedford, lines 43-51)

Donne underscores this cognizance of a gap between mind and object by claiming that trying to crystallize an object for eternity, an
attempt which would imply the acceptance of an absolute standard, was ultimately doomed to failure.

This loss of security would, of course, have a profound effect on the makers of visual images, as it did on the mannerist painters. For, combined with the fact that to Western man the epistemological emphasis had always been a visual one,[23] was the confounding suspicion that the particular was losing its absolute relationship to the abstract. Thus, in Donne's poetry—and to various degrees and with various manifestations in the poetry of the other metaphysical poets—the visual image was no longer able to carry the full meaning it had carried for the poets of the sixteenth century. In many instances, it had no significance except that which man was willing to assign it. It could still represent man's ideas, but there was no assurance that the representations—except when they were of traditional religious symbols—contained either intrinsic or cosmic significance. New discoveries had upset the old relationships between mind and object. Or, as Helen Gardner observed in another context, the division between man and God is overwhelmingly evident in Donne's sacred poetry.[24]

A similar division, although perhaps not so passionately expostulated, exists in the poetry of Herbert. In fact, in his short poem *The Foil,* he laments most emphatically the wideness of the chasm between heaven and earth:

> If we could see below
> The sphere of vertue, and each shining grace
> As plainly as that above doth show;
> This were the better skie, the brighter place.

> God hath made the starres the foil
> To set off vertues; griefs to set off sinning:
> Yet in this wretched world we toil,
> As if grief were not foul, nor vertue winning.[25]

Virtue here is as elusive a quality as it had been to Donne, who could complain that "fluid virtue," in the Platonic sense, gave him nothing positive to work with. But Herbert not only expresses bewilderment that earth reflects so little of the virtue of heaven, he also observes that man is quite apt to misinterpret that which is available to him. Although according to Herbert, the stars, placed at some midpoint between heaven and earth, should give man some indication of virtue as grief should give him some knowledge of sin, man misinterprets the signs; he is capable, in fact, of giving them the opposite meaning from that which had been intended.

Traditionally, of course, Herbert has been regarded as a simple, uncomplicated follower of the word of God, as a man who humbly and unquestioningly pursued the life of a parish priest. But he also is a man who had the Platonic theory of forms sufficiently uppermost in his mind to enable him, in rejecting the secular poetic traditions of the Renaissance, to ask:

> May no lines passe, except they do their dutie
> Not to a true, but painted chair?
>
> *(Jordan I*, lines 4-5)

His skepticism regarding man's ability to arrive at universals as well as his frustration in failing to find concrete forms with which to express his abstract concepts comes out in such passages as,

> O that I could a sinne once see!
> We paint the devil foul, yet he
> Hath some good in him, all agree.
> Sinne is flat opposite to th'Almighty, seeing
> It wants the good of *vertue,* and of *being.*
>
> *(Sinne II,* lines 1-5)

Laurence Howard Jacobs has shown that the poem "poses epistemological problems by noting the inability of man to know what sin is, and by connecting sin to the major means of human knowledge, sight."[26] Jacobs has, in fact, found the problem of knowledge to be a "central and recurrent theme of Herbert's poetry."[27] Herbert's skepticism, Jacobs points out, is evident in such passages as the following from *The Flower:*[28]

> We say amisse,
> This or that is:
> Thy word is all, if we could spell.
>
> (lines 19-21)

His analysis shows that there also is a direct epistemological emphasis, for example, in *Dulnesse, Divinitie,* and *Vanitie* and definite reference to epistemological problems in *The Foil, Artillerie, Providence, The Elixir,* and *The Agonie.* His detailed study of Herbert's epistemological doubts places Herbert decidedly on the roster of those metaphysical poets who were aware of the seventheenth-century's epistemological confusion. Jacobs writes that Herbert's "persistent but unemphatic interest in epistemological problems coincides with the basic insights of Renaissance Pyrrhonism, of Montaigne's skepticism, of Baconian empiricism, and most importantly, with the skeptical faith of Sir Thomas Browne and John Donne."[29] He sees in Herbert's work not only a distrust of the senses, but also an awareness of the inadequacy of language and concludes that to Herbert poetry ultimately "looks forward to the moment when poems cease and God will be seen no longer in the darkened glass of human knowledge, but understood directly."[30]

Thus there is in the poetry of both Donne and Herbert a skepticism toward man's ways of knowing that goes beyond that which was a frequent precursor of religious faith. That their poetry reveals a sure knowledge of the older world view and its epistemological assumptions is obvious. But they were aware also that there *was* an epistemological problem. Crashaw, on the other hand, may not have been; at least there is no significant evidence that would indicate an awareness. However, he may have been responding to, rather than articulating what was occurring. For there is an undercurrent of epistemological confusion in his

O these wakefull wounds of thine!
  Are they Mouthes? or are they eyes?
Be they Mouthes, or be they eyne,
  Each bleeding part some one supplies.
      (On the wounds of our crucified Lord, lines 1 - 4)[31]

The conscious recognition of the problems of epistemology did not stop with Donne and Herbert. Crashaw's younger contemporary, Vaughan, expressed his doubt about man's ways of knowing precisely in terms that had been associated with the emblematic view of the universe. To find answers to the questions of man's relation to himself, God, and the universe, the poet eschews his study in favor of nature itself:

I summon'd nature: peirc'd through all her store,
Broke up some seales, which none had touch'd before,
  Her wombe, her bosome, and her head

> Where all her secrets lay a bed
> I rifled quite, and having past
> Through all the Creatures, came at last
> To search my selfe.
>
> *(Vanity of Spirit,* lines 9 - 15)[32]

Although, in other poems, Vaughan finds spiritual comfort in observation of such natural phenomena as light and waterfalls, here he judges nature incapable of giving him meaningful answers. Having found nature inadequate, he resorts to the *nosce teipsum* solution that had been the basis of Davies' poem on the soul. But whereas Davies observed therein a comfortingly traditional kind of order, Vaughan found what he calls "traces, and sounds of a strange kind." Thus he struggles with the problem of subject-object relationship:

> Here of this mighty spring, I found some drills,
> With Ecchoes beaten from th'eternall hills;
> Weake beames, and fires flash'd to my sight,
> Like a young East, or Moone-shine night,
> Which shew'd me in a nook cast by
> A peece of much antiquity,
> With Hyeroglyphicks quite dismembred,
> And broken letters scarce remembred.
>
> *(Ibid.,* lines 17 - 24)

To examine nature, and even to seek sealed knowledge that had not been previously revealed, was nothing out of the ordinary. Nor was the return to oneself. For, although man's senses were dull and his mind lacking in perfection, knowledge was still possible, as Davies so confidently tells us. Traditional concepts enabled one to fit everything together, if not into a complete whole at least into a satisfying approximation. But in this poem Vaughan finds that this is no longer possible. At first he, too, is hopeful that hieroglyphics might contain within themselves, albeit enigmatically, the secrets of the universe:

> I tooke them up, and (much Joy'd) went about
> T'unite those peeces, hoping to find out
> The mystery.
>
> *(Ibid.,* lines 25 - 27)

Spenser, in surveying that which he saw around him, had found security in the belief that when

> . . . this worlds great workmaister did cast
> To make al things such as we now behold,
> It seemes that he before his eyes had plast
> A goodly paterne, to whose perfect mould
> He fashioned them as comely as he could,
> That now so faire and seemely they appeare,
> As nought may be amended any wheare.
>
> *(An Hymne in Honour of Beautie,* lines 29 - 35)

Vaughan, however, does not find an eternal pattern. He even suspects the validity of the very symbols that would enable him to infer that an eternal pattern existed. At his disposal are neither the Neoplatonic concept, found in Spenser's *Fowre Hymnes,* that earthly beauty is an intimation of eternal perfection nor the Hermetic concept that the objects of this earth partially reveal eternal mysteries.[33] Vaughan finds that he cannot bring the hieroglyphics into any meaningful order and that

> . . . this neer done,
> That little light I had was gone:
> It grieved me much.
>
> *(Vanity of Spirit,* lines 27 - 29)

It is not only what he says, but also Vaughan's selection of imagery that is important, for during the Renaissance "hieroglyphs" were regarded as enigmatic earthly manifestations of the secrets of the universe. Thus he indicates his awareness that there was an epistemological problem that had not been resolved.

While Vaughan could dismiss the problem with a wistful acknowledgment of the traditional answer — that on earth man's means of knowing were necessarily limited — Traherne found its resolution crucial. One of the major questions with which Traherne struggled was that of how the finite mind could know the infinity of God. His answer, which glances forward to the eighteenth century as well as backward toward the sixteenth, suggests that one could expect his visual imagery to be strikingly different from the conceited imagery of the earlier metaphysical poets. He opens his *Centuries* with an inward look:

An Empty Book is like an Infants Soul, in which any Thing may
   be Written. It is Capable of all Things, but containeth Nothing.
I hav a Mind to fill this with Profitable Wonders.[34]

   The "Profitable Wonders" with which he ultimately attempts to
fill the infant soul are emphatically drawn from observation:

A Wide Magnificent and Spacious Skie,
So rich tis Worthy of the Deitie,
Clouds here and there like Winged Charets flying,
Flowers ever flourishing, yet always Dying,
A Day of Glory where I all things see,
As twere enriched with Beams of Light for me.

(Nature, lines 53 - 58)

   If we regard Traherne's lines in the light of the visual images
created by Donne, Herbert, and Crashaw — or even occasionally
by Vaughan — what strikes us immediately is that it is the natural
world itself to which Traherne turns in his struggles to understand
his relation to the universe. It is precisely by observing the glory of
God's creation and emphasizing the knowledge obtained through
such sensory experience that Traherne develops his theory of the
soul's relation to infinity. This is much closer to Locke's corollary
to the concept of the *tabula rasa* than anything the other
metaphysical poets conceived. Locke claimed that "the visible
marks of extraordinary wisdom and power appear so plainly in all
the works of creation" that the seriously reflecting man could not
miss "the discovery of a deity" simply by looking around him.[35]
   Traherne was not even considering the broken hieroglyphs of
which Vaughan complained. Yet the overall world view that those
hieroglyphs represented was something with which Traherne most
certainly had to come to grips. As has been generally agreed, a
strong element of the Platonic runs through all of Traherne's
writings.[36] It was, of course, the inward look that ultimately
became meaningful to Traherne. For, in spite of his assertion that
the infant soul was an empty book, his delight in the sensuous appeal of the exterior world led to the conclusion:

Of it I am th'inclusive Sphere,
   It doth entire in me appear
As well as I in it: It givs me Room,
      Yet lies within my Womb.

(Misapprehension, lines 62 - 65)

Traherne's involvement with "th'inclusive Sphere" provides not only the means whereby he declares his philosophical precociousness, but also the epistemological orientation from which he creates imagery so very different from that of the earlier metaphysical poets. As Marjorie Nicolson has shown, seventeenth-century literature provides a wealth of images that express either a conscious retiring into an inward world or an expanding outward to an exterior world — what she distinguishes as claustrophobia or agoraphobia respectively.[37] Donne, whom one would normally categorize as belonging to the agoraphobics, could, as Toshihiko Kawasaki has shown, wittily challenge a commonplace by depicting the world as the copy of man.[38] His purpose in the following was to present a theory of the expansiveness of man's mind:

Inlarge this Meditation upon this *great world,* Man so farr, as to consider the immesitie of the creatures this world produces; our *creatures* are our *thoughts, creatures* that are borne Gyants: that reach from *East* to *West,* from *earth* to *Heaven,* that doe not onley bestride all the *Sea* and *Land,* but span the Sunn and Firmament at once; My thoughts reach all, comprehend all.[39]

This would at first glance seem quite consistent with the line of thinking that prompted Traherne to write:

The Thoughts of Men appear
Freely to mov within a Sphere
    Of endless Reach; and run,
Tho in the Soul, beyond the Sun.
The Ground on which they acted be
Is unobserv'd Infinity.

(Consummation, lines 1 - 6)

But, as Nicolson suggested, Traherne, ultimately seeks infinity .[40] Donne's thought, on the other hand, springs back upon itself. The mind may be bigger than the world, but like the world it produces "Serpents and vipers" and "diseases and sickness of all sorts." The mind is bigger than the world because of the enormous depravity that it contains. Donne comments:

And can the other world name so many *venimous,* so many consuming, so many monstrous creatures, as we can diseases, of all these kindes. O miserable abundance.[41]

He eventually makes the point that as the diseases of the microcosmic body require a physician, so do the diseases of the soul. He discusses the expansiveness of man's mind for the sole purpose of drawing an analogy. The passage is quite in keeping with the use he makes of most images: it serves as a means whereby he can analyze, in an emblematic way, quite another set of thoughts. However, to Traherne, man's thoughts, moving freely toward the "endless Reach," like infinity itself, seem limitless:

> Extended throu the Sky,
> Tho here, beyond it far they fly:
>   Abiding in the Mind
> An endless Liberty they find:
> Throu-out all Spaces can extend,
> Nor ever meet or know an End.

(Consummation, lines 7 - 11)

The comparison points out a difference in the basic epistemological orientations of the two poets. There is nothing in Donne's words that would on the surface challenge the emblematic world into which he was born. Although acceptance of the older world view is not typical of his writing as a whole, his use of the analogy — even in this reversed form — would appear to be consistent with a correspondence theory of the universe. The same, though, cannot be said about the above passage by Traherne, whose mental wanderings into the infinite are not terminated but, as Stanley Stewart has found, tend to eliminate boundaries.[42] Furthermore, Richard Douglas Jordan has shown that Traherne's comparison of the "Infant Soul" to an "Empty Book" has far-reaching implications. According to Jordan, it was not Traherne's intention that man should either seek infinity through a return to childhood or look for a mystic identification with eternity. To Traherne, he writes, the soul, was endowed with an inner feeling regarding infinity,[43] but was empty at birth,[44] and it was man's prerogative to develop his own faculties to a point at which they, themselves, could become divine.[45] Thus Traherne's epistemological theory, Jordan suggests, is one in which it is experience obtained through the senses alone that enables man to perceive God in the world around him and in history, both secular and Biblical: it is with thoughts gained through sensory experience that he participates in the spiritual "now" of eternity.[46] What becomes really important as far as Traherne's visual imagery is concerned is that he seeks no hidden meanings, analogies or correspondences. The very fact that he fought so assiduously to reconcile Platonism with the concept of a mind that was blank at birth would necessitate his taking a different and more contemporary attitude toward the image. Indeed, there runs throughout Traherne's poetry an exaltation of the senses as a new discovery. In spite of the fact that he could sometimes write of the body as vile,[47] he more frequently lauds

The spacious Room
  Which thou hast hidden in mine Eye,
The Chambers for Sounds
  Which thou hast prepar'd in mine Ear,
The Receptacles for Smells
  Concealed in my Nose;
The feeling of my Hands,
  The taste of my Tongue.
                    (Thanksgivings for the Body, lines 92 - 99)

Thus the physical senses have become to Traherne a much more secure means of knowing than they had been to any of the other metaphysical poets. This becomes particularly important in light of the fact that while all but Crashaw were consciously aware of epistemological problems, Traherne, one of the latest in time, was the only one to resolve those problems into what apparently became for him a satisfactory and complete theory.

More important than any specific theory, though, is what can be concluded from subjecting the metaphysical poets to a scrutiny of epistemological concerns: their awareness of epistemological problems placed them in a position to react to changing concepts of the subject-object relationship. They responded in two ways, both inextricably involved with the metaphysical conceit. The first is that they challenged the medieval concept of an emblematic universe of correspondences; the second is that in doing so they created imagery that was individual and peculiar. Since Samuel Johnson described the metaphysical conceit as a poetic aberration in which the most heterogenous ideas are yoked together by violence, the salient characteristics of the metaphysical conceit have been variously accounted for. Two of the many explanations which are especially pertinent here are Mario Praz's theory that the metaphysical conceit was consistent with the Renaissance emblem[48] and Joseph A. Mazzeo's observation that the metaphysical conceit was based on a "poetic of correspondences."[49] These are not mutually exclusive, for both emblematist and metaphysical poets were heirs — as were all men of the Renaissance — of the medieval belief that everything that existed was linked by universal analogy. What sets the metaphysical poets apart from other poets is the fact that, in consciously or unconsciously responding to the epistemological concerns of their century, they also were responding to the shattering skepticism regarding the concept of universal analogy. They reacted as individuals, but an analysis of their reactions reveals a progression toward a final rejection of that concept by Traherne. Donne and Herbert were already showing signs of unrest by tending to use the psychological remnants of an emblematic universe as a stylistic technique of exploration rather than as an underlying affirmative principle. Vaughan, in keeping with his disappointment in the symbolic hieroglyphs, sometimes even anticipated the next age by drawing his spiritual conclusions directly from observation of nature. Even Crashaw, whose poetry is atypically lacking in epistemological concern, responded to the changing concepts through his intense, almost overstated, appeal to all of the senses.

Certainly, the tendency to try to make their images meaningful in ways that were far from traditional is one of the distinguishing characteristics of the metaphysical poets. But this was not, on their part, the result of conscious calculation; it was their response to the *Zeitgeist,* which had presented them with an almost insoluble epistemological dilemma. For most of them, the skepticism regarding knowledge obtained through the senses, combined with an almost desperate need to visualize, posed a problem that was basic to their creative struggles. Whether the metaphysical poets made direct statements regarding epistemology or not, what appeared to Neoclassic critics as affected intellectualizing was at least partially the result of an epistemological confusion. Presented with a creative problem that was peculiar to the seventeenth century, they solved that problem creatively and peculiarly. For whether or not a creative artist is aware he is doing so, he must operate under epistemological assumptions. He need not be able to articulate an epistemological theory precisely, or even consciously, for those assumptions to play a strong part in the way he presents knowledge to the outside world.

II

"With Hyeroglyphicks quite dismembred"

The tendency to visualize ideas reached its zenith in the early
years of the seventeenth century,[1] and the poetry of John Donne
and George Herbert justifiedly has been associated with the
emblem tradition in both icon and method. But the use of the
emblem by Donne and Herbert was a personal use that denies
rather than affirms the world view that the emblem originally
represented. This is consistent not only with their involvement in
epistemological concerns but also with their relationship to another
aspect of the seventeenth-century emphasis on the visual — the
religious meditation. For in metaphysical poetry, emblem and
meditation meet; and that meeting helped to produce those elusive
characteristics that distinguish metaphysical conceits from the conceits of the Elizabethans.

From the end of the sixteenth century to approximately the middle of the seventeenth, as Louis L. Martz has shown, the continen-
tal meditation had its greatest impact in England and consequently
on English literature.[2] This was also the period during which the
emblem reached its peak of popularity in England. As books of
meditative exercises flooded the English scene, so did emblem
books. England's first emblem book, Geoffrey Whitney's *A
Choice of Emblemes,* was published in 1586; and the popular
Jesuit emblem prints from *Typus Mundi* and Herman Hugo's *Pia
Desideria* were presented to English readers by Francis Quarles in
his *Emblemes* of 1635.[3] Whitney's book was a compilation of
prints drawn from various European sources; and although
Quarles' volume came too late to influence either Donne or

Herbert, the prints themselves were well known before Quarles used them to create one of the most widely-read books in seventeenth-century England.[4]

There are striking parallels between the prints Quarles used and some of the imagery found in the poetry of Donne and Herbert.[5] The interest that Donne and Herbert shared with Quarles in the kind of figurations that appeared in the Jesuit prints is important because the original emblem books containing the prints were among many being produced as part of the Counter-Reformation campaign to compete, through sensuous appeal, with rising Protestantism. Because the emblem of the Counter-Reformation responded to changing attitudes toward the visual image, it provides insight into the kinds of solutions that were made by minds seeking visual correspondences to truth at a time when the validity of such correspondences was being challenged. The metaphysical poets' divergent attitudes toward their visual images reflect the tentativeness and ambiguity of their assumptions about the relationship between man's mind and exterior reality. In that imagery, sometimes even in one image, we can see struggles and uncertainties, the reaching back to what was known and secure, combined with leaps into the new concepts that must have been in the *Zeitgeist*. In their visual imagery, the metaphysical poets responded individually to the confusion attendant upon a culture in the process of moving from the essentially emblematic world into which Donne was born to the far more naturalistic one that Locke greeted a few years before Henry Vaughan's death. The break from the emblematic world is apparent in the poetry of Donne and Herbert; and in Thomas Traherne's poetry it has been almost completed.

The hundreds of books of meditation that followed Ignatius Loyola's *Spiritual Exercises,* writes Martz, utilized the three powers of the soul (memory, understanding, and will) in programs organized into three corresponding parts: composition of place, analysis, and colloquy.[6] In the composition of place, the meditator was asked to visualize the exact spot at which the subject of his meditation had occurred or to find some similitude on which he could concentrate his thoughts.[7] Consistent with this meditative practice and with the focus of the emblem on the emblem print, the metaphysical poets, more often than not, opened their poems as if they had a visual scene or object in front of them.[8]

Sometimes, as Rosemary Freeman has pointed out in relation to Herbert's *The Collar* and *The Pulley,*[9] the metaphysical poem would make no sense whatever if the title did not present the reader with a picture. We, as readers, must *see* the image in the title, *A Jeat Ring sent,* to understand Donne when he writes:

> Thou art not so black, as my heart,
> Nor halfe so brittle, as her heart, thou art;
> What would'st thou say? shall both our properties by thee bee spoke,
> Nothing more endlesse, nothing sooner broke?

(lines 1 - 4)

We must have the image of the ring continuously in mind as we read the poem; for everything Donne eventually says about the unhappy love affair depends on the visualization and analysis of a cheap and worthless bit of jewelry. The metaphysical poet — like both emblematist and meditator — so frequently utilized a picture he apparently had in mind that we, in recalling a given metaphysical poem, tend first to see instead of to verbalize the ideas contained therein. In the poetry of Donne and Herbert, the visual memory of everyday objects — compasses, bubbles, sun dials, buds — is so often a part of the images that flash in and out of the lines we read, that an accurate visual perception of them would seem almost a basic requisite to a full understanding of their significance. Although it is usually the function of such objects that becomes ultimately meaningful — compasses inscribe circles, bubbles burst, sun dials cast shadows, and buds open — our tendency is to see the image before the full import of what the poet is actually doing with it dawns upon us. Complete understanding of the reasoning that was responsible for creating the image comes to us very slowly. We visualize Donne's "gold to ayery thinnesse beate" *(A Valediction: forbidding mourning,* line 24) and Herbert's heart as it is "dipt and dy'd,/ And washt, and wrung" *(Love unknown,* lines 16 - 17) before we are fully aware of the fact that Donne is talking about the two lovers or that the heart Herbert describes is undergoing its tortures as a part of the process of regeneration. What Liselotte Dieckmann has said in her analysis of an emblematic woodcut by Albrecht Dürer is surprisingly applicable: our first pleasure is derived from the fact "that each idea contained in the symbols can flash upon the onlooker's mind, creating a unity of intellectual and aesthetic experience, of sense impression and conveyed thought."[10]

Comparisons between emblem and meditation in metaphysical poetry are similarly applicable. One of Martz's examples of the "composition of place" is Donne's *Goodfriday, 1613. Riding Westward:*[11]

Let mans Soule be a Spheare, and then, in this,
The intelligence that moves, devotion is,
And as the other Spheares, by being growne
Subject to forraigne motions, lose their owne,
And being by others hurried every day,
Scarce in a yeare their naturall forme obey:
Pleasure or businesse, so, our Soules admit
For their first mover, and are whirld by it.

(lines 1 - 8)

It also is possible to point to the emblem in these lines, for the sphere was a common emblematic image. In the first two books of Quarles' *Emblemes,* adapted from the Jesuit emblem book *Typus Mundi (1627),* the globe is the focus of the drama that unfolds in the prints. In one of these dramas, a devil bursts forth from the top of a globe;[12] in another Anima, the human soul, puts her hand inside a globe that represents the world as a hive and finds only wasps, not the honey she had expected.[13] Donne uses this already common image not only as a concrete entity on which to focus his thinking, but also as a point of departure for his thinking processes.[14] But more than this, he implies in the first line that the sphere is something he has somewhat arbitrarily selected; and therefore, using a common emblematic practice, he must prove through analogy that what is true of his vehicle is also true of his tenor. Thus visual similitude enables him to put an abstract idea into concrete form.

Rosemond Tuve, though, in *A Reading of George Herbert,* demonstrated how deeply the images with which Herbert worked were rooted in the traditional sacred imagery of the Middle Ages. Like most writers on Donne and Herbert, she assumed that their universe was the medieval one of universal analogy.[15] Her findings that so many of Herbert's images were common to the medieval period emphasizes their medieval orientation. Earlier she had written that Renaissance images are pleasing because of the mental habit that required both the writer and the reader to see "the intelligible in the visible," a habit which they certainly inherited from the Middle Ages. Her example of this tendency carried to the extreme is the emblem.[16] And, although the minds of both Donne and Herbert undoubtedly were filled with images that they had absorbed directly from medieval texts, they, nevertheless, were at least equally influenced by images as they were used in the emblem books of their own time. For, to an early seventeenth-century poet seeking to visualize abstract conceptions for his meditative composition of place, the emblem would have been the most obvious, the most pertinent, and the most readily available source. Donne and Herbert were living in a world of emblem that had been inherited from the sixteenth century and that would wane as the eighteenth century approached. While they were writing their poetry that world was flourishing most palpably, and its manifestations were everywhere in evidence. Europe's printing presses produced emblem books by the hundreds after publication in 1531 of the archetype, the first edition of Alciati's *Emblematum Liber*. In addition, emblems surrounded Renaissance man in almost every facet of his life that lent itself to visualization. Book colophons, heraldic devices, allegorical figures appearing in the masque, decorations on jewelry, clothing, and household furnishing contributed to the emblematic habit. Joan Evans has shown that Englishmen were, in fact, accustomed to what was becoming a preponderant emblem tradition long before the appearance of the first English emblem book. Mary of Scotland, for example, has left embroidered tapestries that are distinctly emblematic in design.[17] Across the channel, the sixteenth-century French emblematist, Georgette de Montenay, stated quite frankly that she expected the pictures in her book to give woman readers visual ideas for household design along with religious instruction.[18] The craze continued as the Jesuits, before the turn of the century, began to usurp the existing genre in their efforts to woo man through his senses.

If the following lines are any indication, Donne had assimilated the genre thoroughly:

In what torne ship soever I embarke,
That ship shall be my embleme of thy Arke;
What sea soever swallow mee, that flood

Shall be to mee an embleme of thy blood;
Though thou with clouds of anger do disguise
Thy face; yet through that maske I know those eyes,
    Which, though they turne away sometimes,
        They never will despise.
(A Hyme to Christ, at the Authors last going into Germany, lines 1 - 8)

Anyone familiar with the numerous emblem books that came off the presses in the late sixteenth and early seventeenth centuries would recognize the visual components immediately; for Donne not only has used the word "embleme," but he also has used familiar emblem figures. The image of the storm-tossed ship at sea was Petrarchan, but by the time Donne wrote his poetry it had become common in religious emblem books.[19] Hands reaching down from clouds or eyes looking out of clouds had become almost trite emblematic indications of the presence of God.[20] And the minds of Donne's contemporaries would have been storehouses of just such very ordinary pictures gleaned from perusal of the emblem books that were available in the early seventeenth century. An engraver called upon to provide a print to accompany Donne's lines would have had to look no further than the archives of his own art. From the very prevalence of ready examples he could have assumed that he was using a common and accepted visual language. Because of the commonness of that visual language, we, in turn, can assume that these particular lines by Donne were more automatically visual to his seventeenth-century readers than they are to us today. Those readers could not have failed to see — even if Donne had not used the word "embleme" — the basic emblem in the lines. The picture was already in their minds; it was the combination of the components and what was done with them that was new.

Like the meditation, the emblem was essentially three-fold, consisting of picture, analysis of the picture, and moral. But the real significance of Renaissance delight in the emblem lies neither in the influence of the emblem's basic structure nor in the influence of specific icons — although both of these influences certainly exist. The significance lies precisely in the fact that the emblematic was a mental habit which left its mark on the method of image-making.

As initially conceived, the emblem was allegorical, was consistent with the idea of the universe as a series of correspondences, and was associated with Neoplatonism. As Freeman has shown, the emblem reader's pleasure lay in identifying the images that made up the print and then checking his interpretation of the hidden visual statement against what was said about the images in the accompanying emblem verse.[21] That it was the emblem's enigmatic quality that was responsible for much of its popularity is not surprising, for it had been the hieroglyphic interpretation of nature that originally had given impetus to the widespread interest in the emblem. Alciati's *Emblematum Liber* had made the emblem available in popular and fashionable form, but it had not created what E.M.W. Tillyard called "the emblematical way of thinking."[22] The tendency to apply universally symbolic meanings to natural phenomena was a part of the Renaissance's medieval heritage as exemplified by the fable, *The Physiologus* and the bestiary.[23] Sears Jayne points out that all medieval thought up to the twelfth century had been Neoplatonic and that a broad Neoplatonic influence in the Renaissance could have come from such a variety of sources that a work of art could have both expressed and perpetuated Neoplatonism.[24] This would be particularly true of works of the emblematists, who were popularizers and need not have been philosophically articulate in order to have been caught up in the general Neoplatonic view of things. Although all emblematists, certainly, were not directly influenced by the Florentine Academy, there were means of spreading a vague and general brand of Neoplatonic thought sufficient to have helped create a taste for the emblematic.

In its deepest sense, the emblem could be representative of the mysteries of the universe. In fact, E.H. Gombrich writes that the hieroglyphic image neither merely symbolized nor represented the Platonic idea. It was expected to do far more than that:

It is the idea itself, conceived as an entity, which through these images tries to signal to us and thus to penetrate through our eyes into our mind. Put in this form this conception admittedly sounds abstruse if not absurd. Yet it is only the explicit formulation of an idea which is implied in the whole Neo-Platonic approach to the symbol. The very position which regards the symbol as existing "by nature" rather than "by convention" is only understandable . . . if we accept the assumption that the higher orders reveal themselves to our limited mind through the sign language of nature. It is not we who select and use symbols for communication — it is the Divine which expresses itself in the hieroglyphic of sensible things.[25]

Although there were emblems that had nothing to do with either the divine or with occult relationships between image and universal truth, it is this orientation within the emblem tradition that is pertinent here. For it is specifically on this ground that the emblem print and the visual elements of the metaphysical conceit can be at least related to, if not totally identified with, each other.

Dieckmann, who sees the Renaissance interest in the occult based strongly in the Neoplatonic, points to the excitement engendered by the finding of what was supposed to be Horapollo's *Hieroglyphica* and traces that interest back to Plutarch's attempt to explain Isis and Osiris as "tangible representations of universal ideas, as allegories of some philosophical and moral truth.[26] Marsillio Ficino himself, as George Boas has shown, was strongly impressed by the hieroglyph and emblem as sources of knowledge. Boas cites a gloss that Ficino had written concerning a passage from Plotinus. According to Ficino,

the Egyptian priests, when they wished to signify divine things did not use letters, but whole figures of plants, trees, and animals; for God doubtless has a knowledge of things which is not complex discursive thought about its subject, but is, as it were, the simple and steadfast form of it. Your thought of time, for instance, is manifold and mobile, maintaining that time is speedy and by a sort of revolution joins the beginning to the end. It teaches prudence, produces much, and destroys it again. The Egyptians comprehend this whole discourse in one stable image, painting a winged serpent holding its tail in it mouth.[27]

The interest in universal analogy dominates the writings attributed to Horapollo. In them one sees immediately the kind of mysterious, occult objectifications of abstract ideas that make up the emblem prints. In the *Hieroglyphica* we are told that

. . . when they consider the king to be a cosmic ruler and wish to indicate this, they draw the serpent and in the middle they represent a great palace. And reasonably, for the place of the king's palace is the cosmos.[28]

The prints that George Wither borrowed for his *A Collection of Emblemes* (1635) from Gabriel Rollenhagen's *Nucleus Emblematum Selectissimorum* (1611-13) show that the concept on which the *Hieroglyphica* was based persisted well into the seventeenth century. Some of Rollenhagen's prints contain such single

visual statements as Sisyphus' uphill struggle and Ixion's torture
on the wheel. But more typical is a print depicting a griffon on a
stone that is supported by a winged globe. Wither's verse shows
the hieroglyphic thinking behind the images:

The *Gryphon,* is the figure of a creature,
Not found within the Catalogues of *Nature;*
But, by those Wits created, who, to shew
Internall things, *externall* Figures drew:
The Shape, in which this *Fiction* they exprest,
Was borrow'd from a Fowle, and, from a *Beast;*
Importing (when their parts were thus combin'd)
The *Vertues,* both of *Body,* and of *minde:*
And, Men are sayd on *Gryphons* backes to ride,
When those mixt *Vertues,* them have dignify'd.

The *Stone* (this *Brute* supporting) may expresse
The firme abiding, and the solidnesse
Of all true *Vertues.* That, long-winged *Ball,*
Which doth appeare fast-linked therewithall,
The gifts of changing *Fortune,* doe implye:
And, all those things together, signifie,
That, when by such-like *Vertues* Men are guided,
Good *Fortune* cannot be from them divided.[29]

The same hieroglyphic quality appears, for example, in Herbert's
short poem, *Love-joy:*

As on a window late I cast mine eye,
I saw a vine drop grapes with *J* and *C*
Anneal'd on every bunch. One standing by
Ask'd what it meant. I, who am never loth
To spend my judgement, said, It seem'd to me
To be the bodie and the letters both
Of *Joy* and *Charitie.* Sir, you have not miss'd,
The man reply'd; It figures *JESUS CHRIST.*

Herbert's question — stated here so obviously — is precisely
that of the reader of the emblem books: what is the connection
between the emblematic figure and the truth that it both hides and
reveals? The question, although not asked directly, is also behind
such highly visual lines as Donne's,

Our eye-beames twisted, and did thred
  Our eyes, upon one double string.

(The Extasie, lines 7-8)

and Herbert's,

I gave to Hope a watch of mine: but he
        An anchor gave to me.
Then an old prayer-book I did present:
        And he an optick sent.

(Hope, lines 1 - 4)

That connection need not be, and usually was not, an obvious one. For the visual figure was valid to both emblematist and poet if it contained a property analogous to the idea that it was intended to objectify. The method could be used very simply by Herbert:

Mark you the floore? that square & speckled stone,
      Which looks so firm and strong,
            Is *Patience:*
And th'other black and grave, wherewith each one
      Is checker'd all along,
            Humilitie:
The gentle rising, which on either hand
      Leads to the Quire above,
            Is *Confidence:*
But the sweet cement, which in one sure band
      Ties the whole frame, is *Love*
            And *Charitie.*

(The Church-floore, lines 1 - 12)

The poem also serves to illustrate how deeply the emblematic habit was rooted in the medieval heritage. Tuve has shown that Herbert, in *The Church-floore,* used a method that was a part of the medieval tradition. She pointed to medieval sources in which the church-floor had been equated with *humilitas cordis,* the pavement of the spiritual church with the poor in spirit, and the light-transmitting glass of the church windows with the Holy Scriptures.[30]

More frequently Herbert's use of imagery, even though the images themselves were a part of the medieval tradition, approaches the complexity that is evident in *Love-Joy.* And this complexity bears a greater relationship to the *Hieroglyphica,* which was so popular during the Renaissance, than it does to the medieval use of imagery. In the *Hieroglyphica,* we find:

When they with to depict the universe, they draw a serpent devouring its own tail, marked by variegated scales. By the scales they suggest the stars in the heavens. This beast is the heaviest (of elements). It is the smoothest, like water. And, as each year it sheds its skin, it (represents) old age. But as each season of the year returns successively, it grows young again. But the fact that it uses its own body for food signifies that whatever things are generated in the world by Divine Providence are received back into it by (a gradual process of) diminution.[31]

Similar in complexity to Herbert's hieroglyphic grapes is an emblem used by Henry Peacham to objectify the wisdom of Solomon and to apply that wisdom to a person he was attempting to flatter. The print itself shows an eye, a heart, and a crossed cedar and hysop branch over an open book. Peacham says:

The meanes of wisedome, heere a booke is seene,
Somtime the glory of great Salomon,
A Cedar branch, with Hysope knotted greene,
The heart and eie withall, plac'd hereupon:
  For from the Cedar faith the Text he knew,
  Unto the Hysope, all that ever grew.
The eie and heart, doe shew that Princes must,
In weightiest matters, and affaires of state,
Not unto others over rashly trust,
Least with repentance they incurre their hate,
  But with sound judgment and unpartiall eie,
  Discerne themselves twixt wrong and equitie.[32]

The basic emblematic images could be combined to convey messages of varying degrees of complexity. For example, one of the Rollenhagen prints that Wither borrowed depicts a combination of scythe, scepter, and skull.[33] The reader does not need Wither's verses to interpret these images as signifying that even the mightiest will be cut down by death. And if one were to add another symbol — say, the cross — the message would be thereby modified. An example of this kind of modification can be found in Donne's lines:

> . . . I do bring
> The spider love, which transubstantiates all,
>   And can convert Manna to gall,
> And that this place may thoroughly be thought
>   True Paradise, I have the serpent brought.
>
> *(Twicknam garden,* lines 6 - 9)

Donne consciously has added a symbol to modify his meaning. He has used the properties of the visual image, spider, and applied them to the abstract idea of love to indicate love's destructive potentialities. He adds the serpent to show that love can turn a paradise into a potential hell. Sometimes, though, both poet and emblematist would extend their analogies in another way. They frequently let their imaginations carry them much further than a mere one-to-one association of tenor with vehicle or even a composite of such individual associations. They worked on the assumption that if tenor and vehicle were alike in one way, they could also be alike in other ways. Thus almost wild conclusions could be drawn from scant evidence. About the picture of a lone cyrpress tree, Whitney wrote:

> The Cipresse tree is pleasinge to the sighte,
> Straighte, tall, and greene, and sweete unto the smell:
> Yet, yeeldes no fruicte unto the travaylinge wighte,
> But naughte, and bad, experience dothe us tell:
>   Where, other trees that make not suche a showe,
>   Yeelde pleasante fruicte, and plentifullie growe,
> This gallante tree that good, and fruictfull seemes,
> In covert sorte, a kinde of men doth checke:
> Whose curtesie, no man but much esteemes,
> Who promise muche, and faune about our necke:
>   But if wee trie, their deedes wee barren finde,
>   Or yeelde but fruicte, like to the Cipresse kinde.[34]

A comparison of Whitney's verse with Donne's *A Jeat Ring sent* shows how careful both emblematist and poet could be to point out the importance of the exact relationship between tenor and vehicle. In fact, Thomas O. Sloan, discussing rhetorical invention specifically in relation to Donne, carried this idea a step further. "One may go almost as far as to state," he wrote, "that Donne believed a proposition was established if it could be proved by

means of similitudes — that is, if its existence could be tested or ex-
perienced by drawing conclusions from demonstrable relationships."[35] Sloan thus describes precisely the analogical process we
have been talking about. To illustrate his point, he used one of
Donne's conceits — the famous compass image — that certainly
can find no disclaimers to the fact that it is of emblematic derivation:

If they be two, they are two so
    As stiffe twin compasses are two,
Thy soule the fixt foot, makes no show
    To move, but doth, if the'other doe.

And though it in the center sit,
    Yet, when the other far doth rome,
It leanes, and hearkens after it,
    And growes erect, as that comes home.

Such wilt thou be to mee, who must
    Like th'other foot, obliquely runne;
Thy firmnes draws my circle just,
    And makes me end, where I begunne.
                    (A Valediction: forbidding mourning, lines 25 - 36)

"The thought expressed in terms of the compass," writes Sloan,
"becomes a virtual demonstration in which the points of contact
are so carefully drawn by simile that any truth about the compass
can become a truth about his relationship with his mistress."[36] Our
eventual enjoyment of Donne's poem requires that we accept his
contention that souls logically can be related to compasses.

However, it is what Donne and Herbert ultimately did with the
emblematic that is relevant to the visual aspects of the
metaphysical conceit. There is, for example, a decided difference
between Donne's conceit in which eye-beams thread themselves on
a double string and the following visual comparison:

Then all your beauties will bee no more worth
Then gold in Mines, where none doth draw it forth;
And all your graces no more use shall have
    Then a Sun dyall in a grave.
                    (The Will, lines 48 - 51)

Both, basically, are emblematic. But the last quoted could have been used by Philip Sidney, by Edmund Spenser, or by poets whose work was included in any sixteenth-century sonnet series, while this is not true of the eye-beams conceit; nor is it true of such visualizations as Herbert's,

> My soul will turn to bubbles straight,
> And thence by kinde
> Vanish into a winde,
> Making thy workmanship deceit.

(Nature, lines 9 - 12)

We are asked in Donne's passage from *The Will* to see the relationships between beauties and gold that remains in the mine and between graces and the ineffectualness of a sun dial placed where there is no sun. To see a relationship we must see a picture; but it is a static picture. In the passages referring to eye-beams and bubbles the images have been subjected to changes as they pass through the meditating mind of the poet. He has taken liberties with them. Although the conjunction of eye-beams was common in Renaissance emblematic imagery, Donne has made that picture active through the use of the verbs "twisted" and "did thred." Herbert's symbolic bubble performs in our minds as would the real bubble.

It is precisely in this respect that we can begin to see a difference between the emblematic visualizations of Donne and Herbert and those of the poets of the earlier Renaissance. In seeking the cause of this difference, we must take two factors that are peculiar to the early seventeenth century into consideration. The first is the sophistication that such epistemologically oriented poets as Donne and Herbert naturally would bring to the visual image. The second is the effect of the meditative practice itself. For when skepticism as to man's ways of knowing is combined with the meditative practice of subjecting the emblem to the understanding, strange things begin to happen to that emblematic picture to which the poet sought to relate his ideas. The emblem, without losing either its enigmatic appeal or its allegorical base, could become a far more personal means of expression.

The difference that is thereby produced can be illustrated by two highly visual conceits, one by Spenser and one by Donne. The first is the enigmatic Cupid that Spenser's Britomart saw in the House of Busirane; the second is the equally enigmatic conceit with which Donne complicates *The Canonization*. These specific passages serve our purpose particularly well because their emblematic antecedents have been adequately documented. Spenser presents us with a picture that needs to be "read" in order to be understood:

Blyndfold he was, and in his cruell fist
A mortall bow and arrowes keene did hold,
With which he shot at randon, when him list,
Some headed with sad lead, some with pure gold;
(Ah! Man, beware how thou those dartes behold.)
A wounded dragon under him did ly,
Whose hideous tayle his lefte foot did enfold,
And with a shaft was shot through either eye,
That no man forth might draw, ne no man remedye.

(The Faerie Queene, III, xi, 48)

To "read" Spenser's emblem, one must have recourse to the emblems of the period. The knowledge that these emblems give us — and that knowledge would have been readily available to Spenser's contemporaries — endows Spenser's Cupid with a frightening message that is not readily apparent to the modern reader. In the first place, the blindfold itself did not signify to the Renaissance reader simply that love is blind; but, as Erwin Panofsky has shown, the blindfold placed him in the company of such personages as Night, Death, the Synagogue, and Infidelity.[37] The arrows that he holds also add to the meaning, for leaden arrows were destructive; golden, benevolent.[38] Thus Cupid becomes a being of ambiguous potential. It is, though, by tracing the dragon on which Cupid stands directly to an emblem by Alciati himself that C.S. Lewis was able to extract the full meaning of Spenser's emblem. Alciati's emblem, which Lewis found was so well-known that it was actually Spenser's probable source, shows the virgin goddess, Minerva, with a dragon as her attendant. Lewis, therefore, interprets the image to imply that Chastity's guardian, blinded by Cupid's shafts, "has been mutilated at the very organs which qualify it for guardianship."[39] To thus interpret Spenser's wounded dragon, Lewis has had to seek out the specific meanings attached to the symbolic language Spenser employs. And we, to adequately interpret the total passage, also must have access to specific sources within the Renaissance emblem tradition. Because one must "read" its visual elements, Spenser's image is essentially literary, as were the actual emblems that inspired it. This literary characteristic becomes far more complex in what Josef Lederer has called the "cluster of more or less commonplace images"[40] upon which interpretation of the following passage from Donne's *The Canonization* ultimately depends:

Call us what you will, wee are made such by love;
    Call her one, mee another flye,
We'are Tapers too, and at our owne cost die,
    And wee in us finde the'Eagle and the Dove.
    The Phoenix ridle hath more wit
      By us, we two being one, are it.
So to one neutrall thing both sexes fit,
    Wee dye and rise the same, and prove
    Mysterious by this love.

(lines 19 - 27)

To be sure, these images rank among the most common of the figures that were contained in the memories of readers of emblem books. The phoenix, certainly, had been ubiquitous in Renaissance imagery, both sacred and profane. Dove and eagle were, as Donald L. Guss has pointed out, capable of sustaining various interpretations even in the Renaissance.[41] A more precise derivation can be found within the emblem tradition for the lines that bring tapers and flies into such inauspicious proximity to one another. They represent one of those figurations that Praz said went from poetry to emblem and back again.[42] The particular passage that provided the inspiration is the line, "Cosi di ben amar porto tormento" from Petrarch's *Il Canzoniere*.[43] The seventeenth-century Dutch emblematist, Daniel Heinsius, quoted the line in his *Emblemata Amatoria* as an obvious motto for his print that depicts a large candle surrounded by flies and flanked on one side by a pair of lovers and on the other by a lone lover about to stab himself.[44] Another of Donne's Dutch contemporaries, Otho Vaenius, shows a Cupid, bow and arrow in hand, intently watching moths or butterflies encircle a lighted candle.[45] And the same theme, with lovers themselves rather than Cupid, would appear again in Wither's *A Collection of Emblemes*.[46] The specific visualization of Petrarch's line had become common in emblem literature long before it was used by Donne, Heinsius and Vaenius. Whitney had chosen a similar print — with gnats rather than flies — under the motto "In amore tormentum" and with the quotation from Petrarch as a subsidiary motto within the print itself.[47] Exercising the emblematist's right to borrow with impunity, he had compiled his collection from prints that had been used previously in European emblem books; a print indentical to the one described above had appeared in Hadrianus Junius' *Medica Emblemata*[48] and similar figures in *Hecatomographia* by Giles Corozet and *Le Sententiose Impresse* by Paolo Giovio and Gabriel Symeoni.[49] Thus to both Donne and his seventeenth-century readers the "cluster" of images would have been at once less cryptic and more visual than they appear today. The image immediately would have brought to mind the pictures they had seen of insects flying dangerously close to candles; and the mind automatically would have interpreted these as warnings of how dangerous falling in love could be.

But, even with the emblematic source materials at hand, we cannot be immediately certain just what Donne meant by his use of tapers and flies. Spenser had constructed his emblem from images that long had been established in the tradition, and he used them essentially as they always had been used. Donne, on the other hand, takes much more liberty with his use of imagery. He is aware of traditional meanings, but he does not feel that he must adhere to those meanings as precisely as Spenser did. Spenser, more faithfully than Donne, assumed that the images that made up his Cupid were universal and that he needed only to depict them in order to enable the reader to comprehend their meanings and thereby construct his message. His images are enigmatic on the surface but, like Caesare Ripa's *imagini,* are backed by specific meanings accessible to those with sufficient learning to understand them. Blindfold, leaden arrows and golden arrows — all have definite meanings that can be added up to reveal a specific message. Donne's images are enigmatic, too, but differently so. The enigmatic quality in his passage comes not so much from the icons themselves as from the use he has made of them. Our knowledge of possible sources helps us to elucidate his meaning, but it does not completely clarify the passage; for Donne has played with and reinterpreted his symbols. The individual images that make up Spenser's Cupid stand like static hieroglyphs in a

universe in which everything has a hidden meaning. Donne's images have been moved around in his own mind and placed in new
and witty relationships to each other. He has moved away from
the traditionally enigmatic meanings that the sixteenth-century
emblematists had associated with these images; in doing so he suggests that, to him, their significance is not universal, but personal.
He forces the images to contribute to his own expression of the
dual mysteries of man's secular and religious loves. He has, thus,
challenged the images' validity as analogous to anything other than
his own observations.

There is, in fact, evidence within the emblematic tradition itself
that the acceptance of the hieroglyphic validity of the visual image
was wavering. Wither, writing shortly after Donne's death, was
quite aware that his means of expression had become somewhat
shabby; he felt that he had to apologize for the borrowed prints
that made up his emblem book. In dedicating his volume to
Charles I and Henrietta Maria, he was careful to indicate that his
aim was not to please the elite or educated; rather, the intention of
his book was "to please / And profit vulgar Judgments."[50] He did
not hesitate to express his utter lack of interest in the actual
hieroglyphic meaning of the symbols about which he was writing.
One of Rollenhagen's emblems, a particularly enigmatic one,
depicted a crown, a cross and a sphere suspended over three inter-
twined crescents. Before giving his own interpretation of the print,
Wither wrote:

What in this *Emblem,* that mans meanings were,
Who made it first, I neither know nor care;
For whatsoere, he purposed, or thought,
To serve my *purpose,* now it shall be taught.[51]

He had rejected the close association of symbol and meaning that
had been assumed by Spenser and the early emblematists. His
relegation of the emblem to a popular and therefore somewhat
suspect place in the literary scene was symptomatic of the fact
that,by the time he wrote, serious emblems were no longer used
primarily to popularize ethical commonplaces.

By 1635, the year in which Wither's volume was published, the
seriously-oriented emblem had been used for more than half a century as an aid to religious meditation. For some time there had

been, in fact, a dichotomy in opinion as to just what the emblem was. Bacon, as could be expected, had completely ignored the emblem's occult and hieroglyphic potentialities. He regarded the emblem as simply an aid to memory.[52] But in the seventeenth century Quarles still could write of the "Hieroglyphicks and Emblemes" of the glory of God,[53] and Sir Thomas Browne could regard nature as a "universall and publik Manuscript, written in Hieroglyphics."[54] Thus when Donne and Herbert were writing their poetry, there was a choice as to which concept of the emblem one would accept. Even within the emblematic tradition itself, changes were occuring as the emphasis was shifting from secular to religious. These changes were, in turn, consistent with characteristics observable in the poetry of Donne and Herbert.

In her earlier work Tuve took the position that conceits of all kinds are essentially the same; thus she claimed that there were no essential differences in the conceits of various periods.[55] Indeed, analogy between tenor and visual vehicle — and this is also true of the emblem — is one of the obvious characteristics that all conceits and emblems share. But the nature of the emblem itself, as Freeman has shown, changed around the turn of the century.[56] In the later emblems we find universal analogy, in the sense that it had been used during the Renaissance, becoming less important and other characteristics being emphasized instead. The meditative habit, certainly, was responsible for a part of this change. But the change was also consistent with the seventeenth century's epistemological confusion and with a tendency, prevalent in the other arts, to break the close ties between the mind of man and the mind of God or the universe.

This raises the question of just how the images of the seventeenth century *can* be regarded. Tuve has shown how careful one must be in assuming that an image was original. Her examination of medieval liturgies, books of hours, and other medieval material revealed, in fact, so many precedents for Herbert's most startling images that she has left us with the question of just what was original in metaphysical poetry. Her own answer, in regard to Herbert, was that he gave old images new life.[57]

Donne, whose sermons as well as his poems show that he was quite fond of both words "heiroglyphic" and "emblem," has left one poem in which we can see his mind consciously at work to give new potentiality to a traditional emblem. The poem is the one he wrote to accompany an emblematic ring he sent to Herbert. Elaborating on the ring's emblem, which depicted the body of Christ extended on an anchor, he relates the picture directly to himself. He lets the reader see his thought processes as he moves the images around in meditation. He follows the emblem tradition in starting with a given picture and ending his poem with a moral; the anchor and cross contain parallel properties because to Donne the anchor is a symbol of hope and, through Christ's death, so is the cross:

> The Crosse (my seal at Baptism) spred below,
> Does, by that form, into an Anchor grow.
> Crosses grow Anchors; Bear, as thou shouldst do
> Thy Crosse, and that Crosse grows an Anchor too.
> But he that makes our Crosses Anchors thus,
> Is Christ, who there is crucifi'd for us.
> > *(To Mr. George Herbert, with one of my Seal(s), of the Anchor*
> > *and Christ,* lines 5 - 10)

The moral that he draws from his emblem is not the traditional proverbial *sententia,* but his own:

> Crucifie nature then, and then implore
> All Grace from him, crucified there before;
> When all is Crosse, and that Crosse Anchor grown,
> This Seal's a Catechism, not a Seal alone.
> > *(Ibid.,* lines 17 - 20)

That the picture could serve as a catechism could be said of any emblem. But Donne, in applying his own wit to the images, has moved far away from the traditionally static emblem of the sixteenth century. He probably had in the back of his mind the traditional combination of anchor and dolphin which had served as colophon for the publishing house of Aldus Manutius;[58] or he may have been thinking of the popular serpent and anchor variation. But he expands on and deepens the basic idea. For, in the opening lines of the poem, he imagines that a whole sheaf of snakes formerly had been his family crest; and he plays around with the serpent-sin association throughout the poem:

> Yet may I, with this, my first Serpents hold,
> God gives new blessings, and yet leaves the old;

The serpent, may, as wise, my pattern be;
My poison, as he feeds on dust, that's me.
And as he rounds the Earth to murder sure,
My death he is, but on the Crosse, my cure.

(Ibid., lines 11 - 16)

The serpent in the hieroglyphic tradition usually signified the universe, eternity, or prudence. And in the Biblical tradition, it served not only as Eve's tempter but also as a symbol of wisdom.[59] Donne's snake thus becomes a vehicle for multiple meanings. Here we see movement; and we see change. We see not merely rearrangement and condensation, but we see a willingness to treat universal analogy in a highly original manner. Donne approaches the hieroglyph from an entirely new direction. He does not ask himself what the emblem means traditionally, but what it means to him and, through him, to mankind in general. He consciously changed the meanings of his images by subjecting them to his own thoughts.

In Donne's use of imagery, then, we can see the beginning of a breakdown of tradition that will become progressively apparent as we study the visual orientation of each of the metaphysical poets in turn. Donne, as in the "emblemes" that made up his storm-tossed ship at sea and in his "cluster of commonplace images" from *The Canonization,* has given his emblem a very personal meaning. This use of the emblem is consistent with Guss' observation that many of Donne's more original poems were based essentially on traditional Petrarchan images but that Donne, for his own dramatic purposes, elaborated on the Petrarchan image — frequently in ways similar to those used by the witty Italian Petrarchists — to create poems that were outside the mainstream of English Petrarchism.[60] In Quarles' *Emblemes,* there is also evidence of just such playing around with an image. In this collection the storm-tossed ship image from Petrarch is used twice. The first usage, a religious one, is traditional. In the other, though, Hugo's engraver also has pulled the anchor out of context. It is in the hands of Anima, who is slung over the shoulder of Amor as he trudges up the shore.[61]

If we compare two of Donne's conceits, the basic ideas of which he shared with Vaenius and with the *Hieroglyphica,* we can see precisely the extent to which the personalization of the traditional icon became a part of the metaphysical conceit. Contained within the *Hieroglyphica* is a basic visual idea:

When they wish to indicate a man born deformed, but later taking on a normal shape, they draw a she-bear, big with cubs. For the she-bear gives birth to blood coagulated and thick, and this she later warms in her limbs and thus releases the cubs and brings them into proper shape by licking them.[62]

The symbol usually was used by the emblem-makers as evidence that the attainment of perfection in love required attention and care. Vaenius, in his love emblems, retained essentially the original meaning. His print shows Cupid watching a mother bear lick her half-formed cub, and his verse suggests the appropriate lesson.[63] In one of his conceits based on this idea, Donne approaches the traditional symbol differently, emphasizing the possibility that when improperly nurtured the unformed cub can become a monster:

Love is a bear-whelp born, if we o're lick
Our love, and force it new strange shapes to take,
We erre, and of a lump a monster make.
(Elegie XVIII, lines 4 - 6)

So far Donne has merely played with the image, skeptically challenged its original meaning, and said something new with it. But growing out of that changed meaning is another image with which he illustrates his tendency to use the image for a more dramatic purpose. In a far more subtle allusion to the hieroglyphic bear whelp, he employs the original image merely as a point of departure for a complex analogy that has the human mind as its implied visual setting and takes into account the possibility of the monster's perpetuation through procreation:

Man is a lumpe, where all beasts kneaded bee,
    Wisdome makes him an Arke where all agree;
The foole, in whom these beasts do live at jarre,
    Is sport to others, and a Theater;
Nor scapes hee so, but is himselfe their prey,
    All which was man in him, is eate away,
And now his beasts on one another feed,
    Yet couple'in anger, and new monsters breed.
(To Sr. Edward Herbert. at Julyers, lines 1 - 8)

The image — and this is true also of the visual images in Herbert's poetry — no longer held the secret of God's truth but had become an aid to man's mind as it falteringly tried to express that truth.

If, then, one can call the metaphysical conceit a seeking of correspondences, the emphasis must be placed on the act of seeking. For Donne has stretched the concept of universal analogy almost to the breaking point. In the poetry of Donne and Herbert, one can find example after example of oblique references to common images from the emblems. In their meditative attempts to visualize, they drew from the common storehouse. But they took a fresh and personal look at the images they selected and asked the reader to do the same. Praz suggested that it was in relation to his need for the "certainties of the senses" that seventeenth-century man "took delight in driving home the word by the addition of plastic representation and wanted to transpose the image into a hieroglyphic, an emblem."[64] Donne and Herbert did not merely adapt the images they worked with; they nourished these images in the mind until the images grew into something quite other than what they had originally been. We can think of Donne and Herbert as inheriting from the sixteenth century a vast universe of icons that, like Vaughan's broken hieroglyphs, had come to be of somewhat dubious validity. But these were, certainly, the traditional elements of poetry and as such were intriguing. Therefore the poet could play with them, twist them around in his mind, look at them from all angles, and place them in startling relationships to each other. He could ask himself, for example, what would happen if he *did* bring the serpent into Twickenham garden.

CHAPTER III

"Cannot thy *Dove* Out-strip their *Cupid* easily in flight?"

One of the goals of the seventeenth-century religious meditation was a concentration that would lead to an intensification of psychological experience. The visual orientation in the meditation's composition of place was, perhaps, a logical development of the emphasis on the sense of sight that always had dominated Western concepts of man's ways of knowing. This, though, is only a partial explanation of the visual in metaphysical poetry. A meditator could attempt to place before his mind a naturalistic scene, such as Christ on the cross. Or he could set up an object, such as the cross itself, as the visual subject of his meditation. But these compositions of place would not result in either the kind or function of the visual images that one finds in the poetry of John Donne and George Herbert. Donne and Herbert, beset by doubts regarding traditional ways of knowing, used the emblematic image with far greater freedom than had either poet or emblematist of the High Renaissance. But this still does not explain such images as, for example, Herbert's "The stormie working soul spits lies and froth" *(The Church-porch,* line 76). Nor does it account for the kind of visualization we find in Donne's "Batter my heart, three person'd God" *(Holy Sonnet XIV,* line 1). Although these two images are quite different, there is in both an activity and an intimacy of which the High Renaissance emblem print and visual image were incapable. Both are part of the poet's attempt to intensify his meditation, to relate it directly to himself as he subjects the composition of place to his understanding and tries to give it qualities that, as St. Ignatius Loyola had suggested, would enable the meditator to feel that the meditation was passing through his own heart. This results in a psychological involvement and an immediacy that is as different from the poetry of the past as it would be from the poetry of the future.

The comparative psychological involvement and immediacy in the poetry of Donne and Herbert have long been recognized. James B. Leishman, for example, discussing the love poetry of Donne, observed that Donne had broken tradition in telling us "not what his mistress is like but what it is like to be in love with her."[1] More recently, distinguishing metaphysical poetry from that which directly preceded and followed it, Earl Miner characterized it by what he called the "private mode" that results in a close esthetic distance; this, he writes, contrasts sharply with the remote esthetic distance of Neoclassic poetry and, although less sharply, with the middle distance of that of the High Renaissance.[2] Using Donne's familiar eye-beam passage as an example, Miner wrote that the metaphysical poet moved in closely to both the situation and the subject.[3] We could, in fact, describe metaphysical poetry as Morris W. Croll has described its contemporary, anti-Ciceronian prose:

It preferred the forms that express the energy and labor of minds seeking the truth, not without dust and heat, to the forms that express a contented sense of the enjoyment and possession of it. In a single word, the motions of souls, not their states of rest, had become the theme of art.[4]

But, in the poetry of Donne and Herbert, the reader does not merely watch either the "labor of minds seeking the truth" or the "motions of souls." He does more than that. He involves himself in their actions. When Donne writes of eye-beams that are twisted, we are participants rather than observers much in the same way that we are participants in, rather than observers of, the emblem print. We see, as we would in an emblem print, both the cemented hands and the twisted eye-beams. Donne proceeds to present reflections in eyes, two souls hanging like equal armies, and bodies reclining like sepulchral statues. Thus, we are not drawn into the poem through the description of psychological feelings or states but through the visual presentations of them. It is through the mental process needed to extract meaning from the visual images the poet uses, that we begin to participate in the poem. The process is at least partially an intellectual one; it is the process whereby the reader involves himself in any emblem print to produce the kind of participation he achieves when he reads Spenser's emblematic Cupid stanza.

But visual images in Donne's poem and in Herbert's poems actually require an even more complex involvement. For the seventeenth-century meditator, who was somewhat in doubt about the mind's traditional relation to the absolute, had no secure guidelines to follow as he let his composition of place pass through his understanding. As D. H. Roberts writes, "the poets of the seventeenth century were presented with a perplexing problem as to the relationship between the real and the representational, with the ultimate question being, how can we know the real, and what is its relationship to that which is used to represent it?"[5] When Donne's soul, from its earthly prison of flesh, looked through "lattices of eyes," it was much more on its own than the soul of Davies or, for that matter, those of Sidney or Spenser. But the traditional symbols, although deprived of much of their validity, remained. And the emblematic habit of mind was too much ingrained to be thoroughly discarded. Thus the meditator was faced with the problem of using a traditional method to give traditional images new meaning. The solutions that Donne and Herbert resorted to resulted in the freedom with the visible that we find in their metaphysical conceits.

The emblem itself, as it was being picked up by the Jesuits and turned to religious purposes, was responding to the same cultural forces that were responsible for early seventeenth-century painting. We stand, for example, before Leonardo da Vinci's *The Virgin of the Rocks* as spectators before a wondrous but remote vision. But we become involved in seventeenth-century ceiling frescoes; angels, extending their hands to us, draw us upward into clouds and light that defy architectural boundaries to become as "real" as the clouds and light of nature itself. The beginnings of this mimetic tendency were already observable in the church cupolas of Europe. Neither emblematist nor metaphysical poet, though, had the means to depict the flesh as sensuously as did the painter. The emblematist's art had been, first and foremost, a literary art; it had to be *read* in terms of its hieroglyphs. And the emblem, which had depended primarily on the enigmatic qualities of the hieroglyph for its appeal and consequent popularity, did not follow the general trend toward accurate visual representation until the late seventeenth-century. But neither did it keep totally the particular hieroglyphic quality that had allied it with the correspondence view of the universe. The world that we see in these emblems seems to teeter between the real and the unreal, the hieroglyphic and the natural.

Rosemary Freeman has shown that as the emblem left the ethical or moral sphere for the religious, its means of involving the reader became psychological and dramatic rather than intellectual as the earlier emblems had been.[6] She pointed to the action in the prints borrowed by Francis Quarles from the Jesuit emblem books, *Typus Mundi* and *Pia Desideria.* Most of these prints depict the activities of two doll-like figures, Amor (Divine Love) and Anima (Human Soul). In one of the prints, Anima is seated on a globe in which she can see dimly a beckoning Amor. The psychological effect is enhanced because Quarles' engraver, apparently trying to appeal specifically to English readers, has marked the globe with such familiar place-names as Finchingfield, Rockwell, and London.[7] These were, of course, emblems that originally had been Jesuit; and their relation to the Jesuit meditation is important. Here the love emblem, which was most emphatically turned to religious purposes, is of especial significance.

It is through an examination of the love emblem in relation to the visual images of Donne and Herbert that we can find three visual characteristics that help us to explain some of the peculiarities of their conceits. The first is the visualization of the soul as participant in the religious drama.[8] The second is the interiorization of the meditative image. And the third is the equation of the persona of the poem with the object of meditation. Ultimately these characteristics, further complicated by the freedom with which Donne and Herbert handled the traditional images, could be pulled out their normal contexts and placed in original relationships to one another. The results were responsible for some of the salient characteristics of that kind of visualization that has been called specifically metaphysical.

Amor and Anima, who so endearingly act out the soul's battle in the prints Quarles used in his *Emblemes,* were heirs of the little cupids who, in the secular emblem books, had been utilized to impress upon the reader the truisms of love. Quarles, in fact, writes:

And you, whose am'rous, whose select desires
Would feele the warmth of those transcendent fires,
Which (like the rising Sun) put out the light
Of *Venus* starre, and turne her day to night.[9]

The tendency to associate Divine Love with the secular Cupid
was widespread. Vaenius, who has been mentioned in the previous
chapter in connection with the bear whelp image, was typical of
the creators of love emblems. But although he was not a Jesuit, his
decision to use his originally amorous figures in a religious setting
made him representative of what was happening to the emblem in
the hands of the Jesuits; for, as Mario Praz put it, Ovid had been
"succeeded by St. Augustine."[10] And the religious poets were as
much a part of the theft of images from the Petrarchan-Ovidian
tradition as were the Jesuit emblematists. One need only cite the
English Jesuit poet Robert Southwell's claim that he would
"weave a new webbe" in the loom that the love poets had
prepared,[11] and the young Herbert's question, "Cannot thy
Dove/Out-strip their *Cupid* easily in flight?" ("My God, where is
that ancient heat towards thee," lines 8 - 9) to show that, like the
emblematists, the poets could be quite conscious of their attempts
to effect a change in emphasis. "So will a voluptuous man, who is
turned to God," writes Donne in reference to Solomon, "find
plenty and deliciousness enough in him, to feed his soul."[12] But
preceding even Southwell by more than two decades was the
French woman emblematist, Georgette de Montenay, whose
volume, *Emblemes, ou devises chrestiennes* (Lyons, 1571), contained numerous hearts and the figure of Divine Love, whom she
called "vray amour, ou charite en somme."[13] She was quite frank
about her motivation:

Il est besoin chercher de tous costés
De l'appetit pour ces gens degoustés.[14]

For Montenay's appeal to her readers we need to seek no further
than the Renaissance precept that a didactic work, to accomplish
its purpose, must please. But the later emblematists, as well as
Donne and Herbert, were trying to do more than that. They were
using, whether consciously or not, the language and iconography
of love to draw the reader into their own meditative worlds.

The prints Quarles used represent one kind of love emblem that
is comparable to the visual elements in the conceits of Donne and

Herbert: the visualized soul as participant in religious drama. There is in them — and this serves to reinforce the dramatic action — an additional element that completely destroys the static quality one finds in the more directly hieroglyhic emblems, existing as late as the prints used by Wither which were, in fact, similar to the older ones. These were made up of several enigmatic objects presented against a landscape that served only as a background. In the prints used by Quarles, however, the figures are set into the landscape and interact with it. For example, in a print in which Anima poses as a pilgrim, space itself is emphasized for dramatic purposes. Pilgrim staff in hand, Anima stands in the center of a maze and holds onto a rope by which Amor, who leans from the top of a far-away lighthouse, guides her. In the distance, one can see a figure guided by a dog and another who has fallen into one of the deep chasms that border the maze's path. It would appear that, through its iconography, the print also incorporates the message inherent in the traditionally emblematic image of the storm-tossed ship at sea; the light that Amor holds also is visible from ships that sail toward the rocky coast on which the lighthouse stands.[15] Thus the reader can enter the picture and view his own soul beset not by one pitfall but by many as it travels the dangerous road that leads to salvation. Between the prints that were made up of the static hieroglyphic icons and those that were used by Quarles, one finds a difference in the concept of space comparable to that between a High Renaissance painting and a Baroque ceiling. In the one, subject and background are separated; in the other, they are closely integrated. The hieroglyphs remain in Quarles' prints, for these *are* allegorical pictures and *are* meant to be read. But the snake, which would have been a major visual symbol in the static pictures, now crawls through the landscape — its proper size has been restored — as a part of nature.[16] In metaphysical poetry, the static hieroglyphic quality appears in its pure form when, for example, Donne has his persona step back, analyze the picture of truth on a hill, and conclude that because the way to truth is difficult one must strive to reach it before one is overtaken by death. One easily can see the difference between this and Herbert's "wealth" that can itself climb hills and feel tempests.

It is Herbert's active emblem that presents the kind of picture that is consistent with one of Louis L. Martz's observations on metaphysical poetry. In exploring seventeenth-century poetry in relation to the meditative techniques developed by Ignatius Loyola and other Renaissance religious writers, Martz found that those techniques resulted in an interior drama in which the poet sees his soul as an actor on a stage in the presence of God. He found an apt example that he called "almost too good to be true"[17] in Donne's lines:

This is my playes last scene, here heavens appoint
My pilgrimages last mile.

(Holy Sonnet VI, lines 1 - 2)

The prints Quarles used have become, indeed, the stage on which one can observe the soul in action. A crippled Anima, by means of a walker, takes faltering steps toward Amor, who encourages her.[18] And a trembling Anima is brought by a blind personification of Justice to the judicial bar where Amor sits in front of the ten commandments and writes in a book.[19] The last, certainly, recalls Donne's lines:

Oh my blacke Soule! now thou art summoned
By sicknesse, deaths herald, and champion;
Thou art like a pilgrim, which abroad hath done
Treason, and durst not turne to whence hee is fled,
Or like a thiefe, which till deaths doome be read,
Wisheth himselfe delivered from prison;
But damn'd and hal'd to execution,
Wisheth that still he might be imprisoned.

(Holy Sonnet IV, lines 1 - 8)

In Donne's sonnet, as in the Jesuit prints, we as readers are expected to identify with the action and thus participate in it; as Freeman observed, we are now dealing with a different kind of emblem. When, in the various editions of Alciati, Icarus was shown in the act of careening downward from the sun, or vultures were shown nibbling on Prometheus' liver, the reader was to regard these simply as symbols of man's presumption and take warning. The action itself was not significant and functioned, in fact, in the same manner as a single object such as the serpent of Horapollo, symbol of kingship, or a a single phoenix, symbol of regeneration. The same is true of the more complex emblematic images of Spenser which, like many emblem prints, were a combination of images meant to be read; these symbols essentially were static. In Quarles' prints, on the other hand, the reader becomes involved in the action of a human soul, presumably his own. He is expected to identify with Anima and feel fear and hope as she meets danger or reaches toward salvation. It is not difficult to see the little figures of Anima and Amor engaged in dramatic action in *Love III* by Herbert:

> Love bade me welcome: yet my soul drew back,
>   Guiltie of dust and sinne.
> But quick-ey'd Love, observing me grow slack
>   From my first entrance in,
> Drew nearer to me, sweetly questioning,
>   If I lack'd any thing.
>
> A guest, I answer'd, worthy to be here:
>   Love said, You shall be he.
> I the unkinde, ungratefull? Ah my deare,
>   I cannot look on thee.
> Love took my hand, and smiling did reply,
>   Who made the eyes but I?
>
> Truth Lord, but I have marr'd them: let my shame
>   Go where it doth deserve.
> And know you not, sayes Love, who bore the blame?
>   My deare, then I will serve.
> You must sit down, sayes Love, and taste my meat:
>   So I did sit and eat.

Here is the very action that is typical of the Quarles prints: the welcoming of Anima by Amor, the loving grasp of the hand, and the sitting down at a banquet spread for one lover by another. In fact, Amor woos Anima throughout Quarles' *Emblemes*. For example, in one print Anima weeps while Amor, arm around her waist, tries to draw her away.[20]

Although we do not see the actual landscape in Herbert's poem as we do in Quarles' prints, we do watch the figures act out their drama as if an actual landscape were present. The poem moves from the welcome, through the conversation — this is accompanied by gestures — to the final sitting down to what is usually considered to be the Eucharist. It is as if several of Quarles' prints had been combined.[21] The same is true of the kind of action that one finds in Donne's,

> I runne to death, and death meets me as fast,
> And all my pleasures are like yesterday;
> I dare not move my dimme eyes any way,
> Despaire behind, and death before doth cast
> Such terrour.
>
> *(Holy Sonnet I,* lines 2 - 6)

Donne's entire poem, though, as do most of his other poems and those of Herbert, presents a complexity of many emblematic techniques. Thus few complete poems of either poet are as totally based on the dramatic interaction between two figures as is *Love III.* But one finds passages that suggest such interaction throughout their poetry. The following, which like *Love III* is dependent on conversation, is an Herbertian example:

> Meeting with Time, Slack thing, said I,
> Thy sithe is dull; whet it for shame.
> No marvell Sir, he did replie,
> If it at length deserve some blame.
>
> *(Time,* lines 1 - 4)

Both Donne and Herbert, through the use of techniques that are parallel to those of the emblematists, have at their disposal far more complex methods of meditatively presenting the soul in dramatic action. Perhaps the most easily understood example of what can occur as the poet tries to draw the reader into his own meditative world is what happens to the traditional personification. As in Quarles' *Emblemes,* a personification can take on any number of roles with which the reader can identify his own soul or in which he can see his soul's friends and adversaries. The personification of the soul itself as an actor in the drama can be related to Quarles' Anima when it appears in Herbert's poetry in such lines as "Poore silly soul, whose hope and head lies low . . ." *(Vanity II,* line 1). In Quarles' prints one can see, for example, the figure of Anima hanging her head as she is brought before the bar of justice.[22] Encouraging the image to thus develop a personality of its own was a significant development in both the emblem print and in the images of Donne and Herbert. Freeman has shown that

in the seventeenth-century emblem symbols themselves have
become participants in the dramatic action. For example, Occasion — who, in the earlier emblems, would have stood alone with
only her pictured attributes guiding the reader to the moral lesson
— now acts out the role herself.[23] Similarly Donne's Death has
been endowed with life:

Death be not proud, though some have called thee
Mighty and dreadfull, for, thou art not soe,
For, those, whom thou think'st, thou dost overthrow,
Die not, poore death, nor yet canst thou kill me.
(Holy Sonnet X, lines 1 - 4)

Donne's opening lines assume a picture of Death consistent with
the personifcations of death in the emblem prints. In fact, it is
almost as if he were addressing one of the many figures of Death as
powerful skeleton who, in the emblem books, stands ready to part
man from his worldly possessions.[24] Having referred to the picture
before him, Donne proceeds to draw intellectual conclusions. But
Herbert, in addressing his personification of death, goes much further. He gives Death decidedly sensual human characteristics when
he writes:

Death, thou wast once an uncouth hideous thing,
                Nothing but bones.
(Death, lines 1 - 2)

He makes his statement by elaborating on those human
characteristics themselves:

But since our Saviors death did put some bloud
                Into thy face;
        Thou art grown fair and full of grace,
Much in request, much sought for as a good.
(Ibid., lines 13 - 16)

It is much the same thing that Donne, in a secular context, does
to Cupid:

To what a combersome unwieldinesse
And burdenous corpulence my love had growne,

But that I did, to make it lesse,
    And keepe it in proportion,
Give it a diet, made it feed upon
That which love worst endures, *discretion.*

(Loves diet, lines 1 - 6)

Love, here, is not treated as the traditional Cupid which one finds in Alciati and which Spenser, using the method of the early emblematists, had depicted. Human attributes, as in Herbert's *Death,* have been substituted for hieroglyphic ones. What is original in the treatment of the personification by Donne and Herbert, though, is not simply that the personification has been given human characteristics. Spenser, for example — and he was following an older tradition — could write of his Gluttony:

His belly was upblowne with luxury,
And eke with fatnesse swollen were his eyne;
And like a crane his necke was long and fyne
With which he swallowed up excessive feast,
For want whereof poor people oft did pyne.

(The Faerie Queene, I, iv, 21)

But obesity is appropriate to the personification of gluttony; and, therefore, although swollen eyes and a long neck are human characteristics, they serve as static hieroglyphic attributes. Herbert's Death, through the blood of redemption, can grow attractive and healthy; Donne's Cupid can eat and grow fat and, when denied food, become thin again. Health is not relevant to the traditional personification of death; nor is obesity relevant to the personification of love. But, more importantly, both Herbert's Death and Donne's Cupid are capable of change. Donne and Herbert have sought to find meaningful variations on what would have been, in the sixteenth century, a static image. Herbert, in fact, further involves the "Poore silly soul, whose hope and head lies low" of *Vanitie II* when he ends the poem with this active image which also, incidentally, presents the emblematic moral:

Then silly soul take heed; for earthly joy
Is but a bubble, and makes thee a boy.

(lines 16 - 17)

This attempt to humanize a personification can result, as it does in Herbert's poetry, in numerous and various manifestations. A soul can wear clothes *(The Church-porch,* line 146); "proud knowledge" can "bend & crouch" *(Faith,* line 31); or the "merrie world" can,

> With his train-bands and mates agree
> To meet together, where I lay,
> And all in sport to geere at me.
>
> *(The Quip,* lines 1 - 4)

Passing through the meditating mind of Donne, the Petrarchan personification of love can become a very active personage, indeed:

> Yet lies not Love *dead* here, but here doth sit
>   Vow'd to this trench, like an *Anchorit.*
> And here, till hers, which must be his *death,* come,
>   He doth not digge a *Grave,* but build a *Tombe.*
> Here dwells he, though he sojourne ev'ry where,
>   In *Progresse,* yet his standing house is here.
>
> *(Elegie IX,* lines 15 - 20)

And Herbert also can conceive of Death as very busy:

> Death is still working like a mole,
> And digs my grave at each remove.
>
> *(Grace,* lines 13 - 14)

It was not always the active human figure, though, that played out the drama in the emblem prints of the period. Equal in signifance to the love emblems in which one identified Anima with one's own soul was the cardiomorphic or heart emblem. This was an emblem in which the soul was represented by the human heart itself. In a poem that Freeman traced to the emblem tradition,[25] Herbert lets the heart stand for soul in much the same way that Anima does in Quarles' *Emblemes.* Referring to his Lord, Herbert writes:

> To him I brought a dish of fruit one day,
> And in the middle plac'd my heart. But he
>   (I sigh to say)

Lookt on a servant, who did know his eye
Better then you know me, or (which is one)
Then I my self. The servant instantly
Quitting the fruit, seiz'd on my heart alone,
And threw it in a font, wherein did fall
A stream of bloud, which issu'd from the side
Of a great rock: I well remember all,
And have good cause: there it was dipt and dy'd,
And washt, and wrung: the very wringing yet
Enforceth tears.

(Love unknown, lines 6 - 18)

The poet's heart suffers this and other tortures not as a mere symbol, but as a representative, of the poet's soul. And as a representative of the poet's soul, it is regenerated through a symbolic action, as were hearts in the heart emblems. Like Donne, Herbert has placed his soul on the stage where he, and the reader along with him, can see the heart as it suffers the various tortures and can, by substituting his own heart, feel the pain. The emblematic moral lesson is apparent in Herbert's statement that the painful processes were necessary because the heart had been hard, foul, and dull. It is essentially the same kind of process about which Donne writes:

Batter my heart, three person'd God; for, you
As yet but knocke, breathe, shine, and seeke to mend;
That I may rise, and stand, o'erthrow mee, 'and bend
Your force, to breake, blowe, burn and make me new.

(Holy Sonnet XIV, lines 1 - 4)

Karl J. Höltgen, discussing the parallel between emblem and meditation, has found that the verbs — batter, knocke, breathe, blow, and burn — parallel common visual images in the love emblems of the late sixteenth and early seventeenth centuries. Holtgen found emblematic precedents for the most violent ordeals of Donne's heart in such images as iron hearts being beaten on anvils and hearts being pulverized, burned, and blown upon. Finding emblematic parallels also for the regenerative verbs — breathe, shine, seek to mend, and make new — Holtgen justifies the violence and interprets the poem in the light of the purgation, illumination and unification of the meditative tradition.[26]

The kinds of figurations that are found in the heart emblems are found so frequently in the poetry of both Donne and Herbert that it would, indeed, be almost impossible to believe they did not consciously draw imagery from them. Like the emblem genre to which Quarles' prints belonged, the heart emblem was derived primarily from the secular love emblems. But the use of the heart in religious emblems goes back at least as far as Montenay's emblem book of 1571. Here we can see, among other heart emblems, one in which an iron heart is being drawn by a magnet,[27] and another in which a woman drags a heart behind her as she holds her tongue in her hand.[28] The depiction of the heart's experiences, however, took many forms in the religious emblem books. Of that variety of forms, Daniel Cramer's *Emblemata Sacra* presents an excellent example. Shown therein is a heart being beaten by a hammer held by a hand — a typical image, usually regarded as the hand of God — extending from the clouds.[29] And there are others in which the extended hand also plays an important role: it writes "Jesu" on a heart; it squeezes the juice of grapes onto a heart that has been shot with arrows; it holds the key to a lock that keeps a heart chained to a chest of gold; it cuts a winged heart loose from the world; it catches a heart on a fishline; and it shoots arrows into a heart. Cramer hearts are nailed to the cross, shoveled into the furnace, battered in stormy seas and put through numerous other tortures; one, in particular, posseses an eye; and another has grain growing out of it.[30] In other such series, Benedictus van Haeften[31] and later emblematists, such as Francesco Pona,[32] also put the heart through a variety of strange adventures. These, for the most part, are hieroglyphic in concept — although Haeften combines the cardiomorphic emblem with the figures of Amor and Anima — and do not make use of the more naturalistic space found in Quarles' prints and in Haeften's later work, in which he uses the human figure to depict a traveller on the way of the cross.[33] Although there is a strong relationship between what happens to the heart in these emblem books and what happens to the heart in the poetry of Donne and Herbert, Höltgen has suggested that in Donne's work we need not seek to correlate a specific poetic image with a specific emblem print.[34] This becomes particularly true when we realize the extent to which Donne and Herbert were capable of taking liberties with both the abstract ideas and the visual images that they incorporated into their poetry. Viewed in the light of how they used these icons, an examination of the seige-of-love images that appear in their poetry is particularly fruitful.

In the poetry of Donne and Herbert, as well as in the heart emblem, heart imagery serves essentially the same purpose as does the figure of Anima in Quarles' prints; it becomes the reader's own soul and thus functions as a means of intensification. In other words, it woos the reader into participation. But, for the most part, he is not asked to think of himself, for example, as a soul beset by dangers but as a soul that is actually feeling the results of those dangers. One of Quarles' emblems depicts Anima crouching at the entrance to a cave. The usually loving Amor is presented as wrathful and flies above Anima with what would appear to be lightning clutched in his hand. An animal, presumably a fox, crouches at another entrance to the cave while, beside Anima, a snake makes its exit.[35] The picture is one of foreboding, and no more than that. For in most of Quarles' prints, evil can still be averted and good is yet to be enjoyed; basically, his prints are emblems of conflict. In one sense, this may also be true of Haeften's heart emblems. For example, in the presentation of "cordis humiliato," Anima watches the humble heart as Amor squeezes it in a press.[36] In Cramer's emblems, however, the heart alone stands as the focal point and receiver of the action. Thus, although these emblems are hieroglyphic and must be read in the same way as George Wither's emblems, for example, must be read, they nevertheless provide for the meditating reader a means of identification which is not only different, but also far more intense than that provided by Wither's emblems. Rarely, and then only incidentally, does this occur in the more naturalistic prints used by Quarles.

Both Donne and Herbert were as capable of using the methods found in the heart emblems as they were of giving life to their symbols. The battered heart — as in Cramer's emblem of the heart struck by the hand of God — and the heart thrown into the font are receivers of the action as well as focal points of the visual image. In an image that recalls Montenay's heart drawn by a magnet, Donne suggests the older and simpler emblematic use of the heart as object of action:

Thy Grace may wing me to prevent his art,

And thou like Adamant draw mine iron heart.

(Holy Sonnet I, lines 13 - 14)

And Herbert can mildly, and somewhat obliquely, complicate the basic image:

Onely God, who gives perfumes,
            Flesh assumes,
And with it perfumes my heart.

(The Banquet, lines 22 - 24)

He can turn the iconography of Cramer's emblem directly around:

Sinne is still hammering my heart
Unto a hardnesse, void of love:
Let suppling grace, to crosse his art,
            Drop from above.

(Grace, lines 17 - 20)

We participate even more deeply in the poet's meditative experience when, using the second means of intensification they share with the heart emblem, Donne and Herbert interiorize the visual image. In Donne's *The Legacie,* the persona symbolically ripped open his body so that he could see "where hearts did lye" (line 14) and then complained of what he found there. Similarly in *The Dampe* (lines 1 - 4), an autopsy will reveal the mistress' picture in the heart of the dead lover. The peculiar use to which Donne has put the heart imagery here is obviously different from that in which the heart is made the recipient of punitive regeneration. Here it is used as a means of interiorization of the action or thought; this is the use to which Donne put the second of his bear whelp images when he referred to the mind as a theater. Again, in this interiorization, metaphysical conceit meets with meditation and emblem. But the root of such interiorization is traditional, for it had been inherent in medieval associations of love and religion. For example, in the following medieval lyric, Christ, as lover, pleads that the locked door of the soul-as-bride may be opened for him:

Undo thy door, my spouse so dear,
Alas! why stand I locked out here?

I am thy Lord to take.
Look at my locks and at my head,
And all my limbs with blood o'erspread
    For thy sake.[37]

In the seventeenth century, the Dutch engraver Antonius
Wiericx could depict Jesus on the outside of a most enlarged and
somewhat realistic heart. In one emblem print, Christ, carrying the
cross, approaches a large heart surrounded by clouds; and in
another, he stands on a cloud as he seeks the handle of the heart's
door.[38] However the Wiericx series, *Cor Jesu Amanti Sacrum,* carries the basic idea further, directly into the kind of interiorization
that Donne suggests when his persona finds a picture in his heart
or when the mind becomes a theater. For Donne was emphasizing
an aspect of the religious meditation that was, most certainly, applicable to his poetry. But it was even more pertinent to the poetry
of Herbert. "Essentially the meditative action," writes Martz,
"consists of an interior drama in which man projects a self upon
an interstage, and there comes to know that self in the light of a
divine presence."[39] The Wiericx prints bring that interior drama to
actual visualization, for Wiericx uses a series of prints in which the
heart's interior serves as a stage for the battle of Christ against the
forces of evil. Onto this heart-stage, Christ is seen carrying a
lantern to reveal infesting snakes and other evil creatures. Subse-
quently, he is depicted sweeping the heart with a broom, washing
it, and finally, after a number of other activities, enthroning
himself there.[40] The similarity in the concept behind the Wiericx
prints and that employed by Herbert in, for example, *Good Friday*
is striking. Herbert asks himself how he can measure the redemptive blood of Christ. And he answers himself thus:

Since bloud is fittest, Lord, to write
Thy sorrows in, and bloudie fight;
My heart hath store, write there, where in
One box doth lie both ink and sinne:

That when sinne spies so many foes,
Thy whips, thy nails, thy wounds, thy woes,
All come to lodge there, sinne may say,
No room for me, and flie away.

Sinne being gone, oh fill the place,
And keep possession with thy grace;
Lest sinne take courage and return,
And all the writings blot or burn.

(lines 21 - 32)

Herbert — more frequently than Donne — is capable of a number of highly original variations on the theme. In *Decay,* for example, "some one corner of a feeble heart" becomes a battleground

Where yet both Sinne and Satan, thy old foes,
Do pinch and straiten thee, and use much art
    To gain thy thirds and little part.

(lines 12 - 15)

His poem *Jesu* shows the persona fitting together the pieces of a puzzle within the heart's interior:

JESU is in my heart, his sacred name
Is deeply carved there: but th'other week
A great affliction broke the little frame,
Ev'n all to pieces: which I went to seek:
And first I found the corner, where was *J,*
After, where *ES,* and next where *U* was graved.
When I had got these parcels, instantly
I sat me down to spell them, and perceived
That to my broken heart he was *I ease you,*
      And to my whole is *JESU.*

Thus the Ignation admonition that the meditator attempt to feel the subject of the meditation passing through his own heart could result in quite literal manifestations in both metaphysical poetry and the emblem.

The third means of intensification, equating the poem's persona with the object of meditation, also can be illustrated by reference to the emblem tradition. Josef Lederer, in his discussion of the emblematic in relation to the poetry of Donne, reproduces a print that appeared in one of the editions of Loyola's *Spiritual Exercises.* The print shows a human figure pierced by a number of swords; each of the swords represents a vice that threatens man's soul.[41] And again, the emblem brings to actual visualization a

characteristic of the poetry of Donne and Herbert— in this case
the equating of the persona of the poem with the object of meditation. For we find in their poetry a number of passages, and
sometimes entire poems, in which the action of the symbols is
directed toward the poem's persona. The whole of Donne's
Twicknam Garden, for example, is based upon this principle.
Donne opens the poem with the persona as the center of a landscape with which the persona will ultimately become totally involved:

Blasted with sighs, and surrounded with teares,
   Hither I come to seeke the spring,
   And at mine eyes, and at mine eares,
Receive such balmes, as else cure every thing.

(lines 1 - 4)

The action that follows takes place in an emblematic setting to
which Donne adds a spider and a serpent that contribute to the
personal meaning of the landscape. And it is in this personalized
setting that the persona, himself, eventually becomes an actual
emblem:

Love let mee
   Some senslesse peece of this place bee;
Make me a mandrake, so I may groane here,
Or a stone fountalne weeping out my yeare.

Hither with christall vyals, lovers come,
   And take my teares, which are loves wine,
   And try your mistresse Teares at home,
For all are false, that tast not just like mine.

(Ibid., lines 15 - 22)

There is an emblematic tradition for such fountains that goes
back at least as far as Montenay and that also appears in Quarles'
Emblemes. In some of the editions of Montenay's series, the
wounds of Christ, who stands as the center of the fountain, send
forth the redemptive blood which is eagerly sought by the human
figures at the fountain's base.[42] But a clearer example of the identification of self with the objectification of an abstract idea can be
found in one of Quarles' prints, which depicts two Animas. One

has become a fountain with water flowing from her hands; the other, sitting before her own image as fountain, clasps her hands while Amor, from the sky, pours water on her head. The accompanying quotation — "O that my Head were waters, and mine eyes a fountaine of teares"[43] — underlines the fact that the source of much of this kind of imagery was originally Biblical. Emblematic parallel, however, is not as important as the turn of mind that was responsible for such figurations. That Donne was quite aware of what he was doing is evident in the following:

This twilight of two yeares, not past nor next,
   Some embleme is of mee, or I of this,
Who Meteor-like, of stuffe and forme perplext,
   Whose *what,* and *where,* in disputation is,
   If I should call mee *any thing,* should misse.
       (To the Countesse of Bedford. On New-yeares day, lines 1 - 5)

Although Donne implies here that the equating of himself with anything exterior would miss its mark, his attempting such equations is, certainly, characteristic of his poetry. Most traditional is his,

I am a little world made cunningly
Of Elements, and an Angelike spright.
       (Holy Sonnet V, lines 1 - 2)

    The equating of the physical world with the human body had its roots in the concept of a correspondence between the macrocosm and the microcosm and, thus, was one of the ubiquitous metaphors of the Renaissance. In Donne's own period, Phineas Fletcher based a long poem on the description of the human body as natural landscape.[44] The metaphor was so prevalent that, as Marjorie Nicolson has pointed out, when Harvey first described the human circulatory system he did so by comparing it to evaporation and rain.[45] But Donne, in *Twicknam Garden,* goes beyond the mere use of correspondence as metaphor. Like Anima in the Quarles print, his persona becomes a specific physical object and takes on the characteristics of that object; therefore it is not man's body but his soul that is equated with the natural world. The persona's soul, physically represented, has become the center of the poem's action. Donne accomplishes the same thing when, for example, he projects himself into his own deathbed scene:

Since I am comming to that Holy roome,
  Where, with thy Quire of Saints for evermore,
I shall be made thy Musique; As I come
  I tune the Instrument here at the dore,
  And what I must doe then, thinke here before.
                    (Hymne to God my God, in my sicknesse, lines 1 - 5)

And the persona himself becomes the "epitaph" of the "yeares midnight" in *A nocturnall upon S. Lucies day, Being the shortest day* (lines 1 - 9). Although Herbert tended to let his persona wander through an allegorical landscape from which conclusions could be drawn, he also was capable of intensifying his poetic statement by letting his persona itself become the recipient of his symbols' action. One of his images — although here the heart is the recipient of the action — is conceptually similar to the emblem from the *Spiritual Exercises:*

My thoughts are all a case of knives,
        Wounding my heart
        With scatter'd smart,
As watring pots give flowers their lives.
        Nothing their furie can controll,
        While they do wound and pink my soul.
                    (Affliction IV, lines 7 - 12)

But in the preceding stanza it is persona as soul that becomes the object:

Broken in pieces all asunder,
        Lord, hunt me not,
        A thing forgot,
Once a poore creature, now a wonder,
        A wonder tortur'd in the space
        Betwixt this world and that of grace.
                    (Ibid., lines 1 - 6)

And in some of the stanzas of *The Flower,* the persona, just as Donne's persona took on the characteristics of a fountain, takes on the characteristics of the meditative object stated in the poem's title:

And now in age I bud again,
After so many deaths I live and write;
    I once more smell the dew and rain,
And relish versing: O my onely light,
          It cannot be
          That I am he
   On whom thy tempests fell all night.

                         (lines 36 - 42)

Perhaps the most direct statement about seeking intensification by
making the persona recipient of the action occurs when Herbert
writes:

O who will give me teares? Come all ye springs,
Dwell in my head & eyes: come clouds, & rain:
My grief hath need of all the watry things,
That nature hath produc'd. Let every vein
Suck up a river to supply mine eyes,
My weary weeping eyes, too drie for me,
Unlesse they get new conduits, new supplies
To bear them out, and with my state agree.

                       (Grief, lines 1 - 8)

What had been a simple microcosm-macrocosm analogy has
become, in the poetry of Donne and Herbert, highly complex and
almost excruciatingly subjective.

   The technique of using the persona as the recipient of the symbols' action, though — along with that of using the symbol as an
actor in the drama and the interior of the heart as a stage — was
brought to further complexity as it was subjected to the meditating
mind of the metaphysical poet. The necessity to dwell on the
selected similtudes of the meditation can account for much that is
strangely visual in the poetry of Donne and Herbert. After Donne
has, for example, called himself "a little world made cunningly,"
divided that world into flesh and spirit, and indicated that both
parts must die because sin has betrayed them, he expands on and
complicates the globe image:

Powre new seas in mine eyes, that so I might
Drowne my world with my weeping earnestly,
Or wash it, but it must be drown'd no more:
But oh it must be burnt! alas the fire

Of lust and envie have burnt it heretofore,
And made it fouler; Let their flames retire,
And burn me O Lord, with a fiery zeale
Of thee and thy house, which doth in eating heale.

(Holy Sonnet V, lines 7 - 14)

Both tears and globes were a part of the emblematic tradition, and both could be pulled out of their normal contexts. In one of Henry Peacham's emblems, an enlarged eye with tears flowing from it is depicted in the middle of the sky. Peacham writes:

Looke how the *Limbeck* gentlie downe distil's,
In pearlie drops, his heartes dear quintescence:
So I, poore Eie, while coldest sorrow fills,
My brest by flames, eforce this moisture thence
  In Christall floods, that thus their limits breake,
  Drowning the heart, before the tongue can speake.[46]

Here the basic image becomes a starting point for the application of its properties to other images. The visualized tear drops become chrystal floods, whose hardness must be broken in order to drown a flaming heart. A more simple, but nevertheless appropriate example is a Montenay emblem in which a hand from the clouds holds a book that, itself on fire, ignites a globe. Montenay's explanation is:

L'Evangile est comme feu estimé.
Car ausi tost que lon va le preschant,
Le monde en est tout soudain allumé.
Mais cela vient de la part du meschant.
Ce feu brulant, glaive à double trenchant,
De tous costez vivement coupe & brule.
De l'une part purge l'or & l'argent,
D'autre il consume & la paille & l'estule.[47]

Donne goes further than Montenay and even Peacham in rearranging his symbols and placing them in new relationships to each other. In *Holy Sonnet V,* the eyes become so large that they can contain seas which can either wash or drown his world. Then, moving back to the globe itself, Donne's mind shifts to another possibility that an emblematic globe could be subjected to — burning. For lust and envy have already burned the "little world made cunningly." And thus, as his mind plays, it exchanges one kind of fire for another; his globe is finally touched, as was the globe in Montenay's emblem, with the fire of religious zeal that contains the paradoxical capabilities of both consuming and restoring. What we see here is the meditating mind, objectifying the subject of his meditation and then, with the visual potentialities uppermost in his mind, placing the original image he had selected in various relationships to other images that he shared with the emblematists. It is this kind of continuous shift of context that is so aptly ex-emplified in *A Valediction: of weeping:*

> Let me powre forth
> My teares before thy face, whil'st I stay here,
> For thy face coines them, and thy stampe they beare,
> And by this Mintage they are something worth,
> > For thus they bee
> > Pregnant of thee;
> Fruits of much griefe they are, emblemes of more,
> When a teare falls, that thou falst which it bore,
> So thou and I are nothing then, when on a divers shore.
>
> (lines 1 - 9)

Similarly, we can watch the meditating mind of Herbert as he at-tempts to visualize the significance of the seventh day of the week:

> Sundaies the pillars are,
> On which heav'ns palace arched lies:
> The other dayes fill up the spare
> And hollow room with vanities.
> They are the fruitfull beds and borders
> In Gods rich garden: that is bare,
> > Which parts their ranks and orders.
>
> *(Sunday,* lines 22 - 28)

The complexity that could result from the combined use of techniques shared with the emblematists can be seen in another stanza from the same poem:

> The other dayes and thou
> Make up one man; whose face thou art,
> Knocking at heaven with thy brow:
> The worky-daies are the back-part;

The burden of the week lies there,
Making the whole to stoup and bow,
    Till thy release appeare.

(Ibid., lines 8 - 14)

Here periods of time are put together to make up a human figure which, in turn, takes on the characteristics of the active symbol. In fact, a symbol which takes on the potentialities of a visual object is capable of almost unlimited variation, a characteristic shared by the emblem prints of the period. For example, one of the prints used by George Wither shows a tongue with wings.[48] Herbert links such seemingly inappropriate images together when he writes,

    Lord JESU, heare my heart,
Which hath been broken now so long,
      That ev'ry part
      Hath got a tongue!

(Longing, lines 73 - 75)

Similarly, Donne can speak of light that "hath no tongue, but is all eye . . ." *(Break of day,* lines 7 - 12). Or Herbert can claim that man has divided the name of God into pieces and thrown the pieces in the dust *(Love I,* lines 3 - 4). And he can, in emblematic fashion, suggest:

Thy friend put in thy bosome: wear his eies
Still in thy heart, that he may see what's there.

(The Church-portch, lines 271 - 271)

Thus, by subjecting their icons to meditative analysis, Donne and Herbert arrived at visual images that could be simultaneously active, interiorized, and acted upon. Although the metaphysical conceit, in its totality, defies precise definition, these visual characteristics most certainly must be taken into consideration. For to the meditator, the setting up of an icon — the composition of place — was only the first step in his attempt to make a concrete picture out of an abstract idea. It is in the progression to the second step, the understanding or analysis, that Donne and Herbert made use of many emblematic techniques, sometimes even combining them to create visual imagery that is typically metaphysical. They could mull the images over in their minds until those images meant exactly what they wanted them to mean. And, like the emblematists who sought to achieve psychological intensity by involving the reader in the drama of the emblem print, Donne and Herbert could involve the reader in a visual drama in which the images themselves participated. For the two poets were writing in a period that demanded both visualization and psychological intensification; they had absorbed all of the visual manifestations of the emblematic tradition and were capable of transforming them into verbal expression. As meditators, they moved the icon through their own minds to achieve a complexity of which the strictly visual medium was incapable. But, nevertheless, they worked within the *Zeitgeist;* for the emblem print itself, in attempting to involve the reader in psychological drama, was responding to the same forces that were affecting metaphysical poetry. In both metaphysical poetry and the emblem, this response to culture forces resulted in an almost desperate attempt to make visual that which has no counterpart in exterior reality. The tongue with wings as depicted in Wither's prints and the heart interior infested with toads and vermin as depicted in Wiericx's are quite consistent with the more complex and stranger of the metaphysical conceits. Emblem and metaphysical conceit produced a visual world in which it does not seem unlikely that a gravedigger might find a wreath of hair encircling the bones of a dead lover or that one might be asked to wear his friend's eye in his bosom.

IV

"Real Crowns and Thrones and Diadems"

Although the epistemology that would give exterior nature precedence over the ideas of the mind would not begin to reach verbally articulate acceptance until late in the seventeenth century, evidence of the final defeat of the innate idea appeared in the visual arts much earlier. In the sensuous naturalism of Baroque painting and sculpture, response to the actual and visibly palpable had superceded the interdependent subject-object relationship of Neoplatonism. The shift in emphasis also is apparent in the visual imagery of the later metaphysical poets. It manifests itself in a progressive rejection of the emblematic. Those peculiarities of metaphoric expression that John Donne and George Herbert shared with the seventeenth-century emblematists and that used the vocabulary of a universe of correspondences while challenging that world-view's validity, tend to become increasingly faint when we reach the poetry of Richard Crashaw, Henry Vaughan and Thomas Traherne. Emblematic elements—the representation of the visualized soul as participant in religious drama, the interiorization of the meditative image, and the equation of the persona with the object of meditation—tend to become less pervasive. For, as the meditator became less mentally involved in the ideal or the enigmatic, emblem and meditation began to lose their close association.

While not directly suggesting an epistemological context, earlier critical opinion on various aspects of the visual imagery of Crashaw, Vaughan and Traherne obliquely supports the observation that these poets were abandoning the inate idea in favor of an increasingly vigorous emphasis on knowledge acquired through sensory experience.

Somewhere near the center of that shift in emphasis lies the visual imagery of Crashaw. The peculiar sensuosity of his poetry represents an ambiguous meeting of two worlds. His visual imagery seems, in fact, to stand almost at midpoint between two concepts of man's ways of knowing. Elements recalling the philosophy of an interrelated universe of correspondences clash violently with a strong emphasis on the senses. It is at least partly for this reason that it has been so necessary to defend what has often been termed the Baroque extravagance of such passages as,

Upwards thou dost weep.
Heavn's bosome drinks the gentle stream.
Where th' milky rivers creep,
Thine floates above; & is the cream.
                    (Sainte Mary Magdalene or the Weeper, IV)

For the worshipful distance that Crashaw sets between us and the object of his meditation prevents us from accepting the emblematic elements of the passage with the same willing suspension of disbelief we accord the interiorized emblematic images of Donne and Herbert. But the emblematic *is* involved in Crashaw's passage. In fact, few writers on Crashaw have failed to note his dependence on the emblem; nor did Crashaw fail to leave primary evidence of his emblematic orientation.

Ruth Wallerstein emphasized the complexity of influences — Baroque synthesis, Classicism, Marinism, meditation, the emblem — that meet in Crashaw's poetry.[1] The format of *Carmen Deo Nostro* underlines the fact that, to Crashaw himself, emblems were to be taken seriously. For it is emblem prints — some hieroglyphic in concept, and some frankly illustrative — which introduce a number of poems in that volume. The epigram preceding the poems indicates that some of the pictures were first "made with his owne hand."[2]

In his work on the emblem, Mario Praz pointed out a similarity between Crashaw's imagery and that of contemporary emblem prints.[3] Austin Warren saw fit to include in the center of his monograph on Crashaw a section that, by implication, placed Crashaw in the emblem tradition.[4] The relationship between Crashaw and the emblem tradition has been studied in detail by

Marc F. Bertonasco, who found actual parallels within the tradition for many of Crashaw's images. Demonstrating that it is the emblematic method of communication in combination with the meditative practice that is important in Crashaw's poetry, he suggests that "the emblematic pattern of most of Crashaw's imagery is the key to its most disturbing features."[5] For the most part, though, Crashaw's emblematic references do not upset our equilibrium as does the conceit on the Magdalen's tears. However, when the emblematic is responsible for twentieth-century uneasiness in regard to Crawshaw's imagery, it is precisely because the meditative orientation of Crashaw's persona is that of a worshiper of an icon and as such does not involve his soul in any kind of emblematic action. How that worshipful distance affects Crawshaw's imagery can be seen when we compare his use of images from love and heart emblems with those drawn by Donne and Herbert from the same sources.

Like the love emblems, Crashaw's poetry draws on the Canticles'pervasive sensuosity;[6] and like the heart emblems, his poetry incorporates siege-of-love imagery. But the siege-of-love imagery he uses does not usually manifest itself in his poetry in the same way as in the poetry of Donne and Herbert. A heart emblem—a print of a heart that is locked—introduces the 1652 edition of *Carmen Deo Nostro;* and the imagery that Crashaw uses in the dedicatory poem to the Countess of Denbigh is that of the siege-of-love. The opening lines of Crashaw's poem, an attempt to proselytize, refer directly to the emblem print itself:

What heav'n-intreated HEART is This?
Stands trembling at the gate of blisse;
Holds fast the door, yet dares not venture
Fairly to open it, and enter.
        (To the Noblest & best of Ladyes, the Countesse of Denbigh, lines 1 - 4)

Although both the heart that Crashaw depicts and the heart of Donne's *Holy Sonnet XIV* are in the tradition of the heart emblem, a comparison of *Holy Sonnet XIV* with any of the lines from Crashaw's poem immediately reveals a difference:

Yeild then, O yeild, that love may win
The Fort at last, and let life in.
Yeild quickly. Lest perhaps you prove

Death's prey, before the prize of love.
This Fort of your fair selfe, if't be not won.
He is repulst indeed; But you'are undone.

(Ibid., lines 63 - 68)

In Crashaw's poem, the elements of the siege-of-love tradition —
darts, wounds, arrows, healing, and even "love's seege," itself —
are there; and the heart becomes a fort. But these images are not
interiorized; for we, like the Countess of Denbigh, can see the picture as we would see the print in an emblem book. But Crashaw
does not, in the same way as Donne, draw us into the picture. We
identify directly with Donne's heart battered upon an emblematic
stage, for he has used the besieged heart image in much the same
way that the emblematists of the period would have used it. But,
although Crashaw uses the same basic theme and its attendant
iconography, we do not feel the darts. He depicts the heart as a
besieged fort, but we do not feel the blows; for Crashaw has step-
ped back from the emblem that precedes his poem. He has not involved himself in it as did Donne and Herbert; he has, in other
words, not interiorized his thought.

Both Donne and Herbert applied the Ignatian admonition to
think of the matter of the meditation as passing through the
meditator's own heart with relative consistency. This is not true of
Crashaw. Crashaw's personna, except on rare occasions, neither
participates in the action nor considers himself, or the representative of himself visualized as heart or soul, as the recipient of the
action. His poetry is not soul-searching, and thus is not dramatic in
the same sense as the poetry of Donne and Herbert. As Bertonasco
points out, Crashaw's emphasis on God's love instead of his power
— an emphasis found in the meditations of St. Francis De Sales —
would eliminate from the meditation the examination of the soul
for evidence of sin.[7] Thus Crashaw's images and his use of them
need not have the purgative intent found in the heart imagery of
Donne's *Holy Sonnet XIV.* The soul objectified, either as personification or as heart, has little place in Crashaw's emblems. Instead, even when he uses the siege-of-love imagery, as he does
again in the following lines, he sets himself apart as an observer.
Although he addresses his meditative icon, St. Theresa, no objectification of his own soul participates directly in the poem's action:

How kindly will thy gentle HEART
Kisse the sweetly-killing DART!
And close in his embraces keep
Those delicious Wounds, that weep
Balsom to heal themselves with.

(A Hymn to the Name and Honor of the Admirable Sainte
Teresa . . ., lines 105 - 109)

Crashaw sets up the visual icon itself as an emblem of worship, a method which automatically would preclude the kind of involvement one finds in the visual imagery of Donne and Herbert. In his other poem on St. Theresa, actually written with a specific work of visual art in mind, Crashaw more obviously establishes this worshipful distance through his address to the reader as observer:

Well meaning readers! you that come as freinds
And catch the pretious name this peice pretends;
Make not too much hast to'admire
That fair-cheek't fallacy of fire.

(The Flaming Heart . . ., lines 1 - 4)

He enters his emblems only to the extent that one watching a film can participate in the action:

Run MARY run! Bring hither all the BLEST
ARABIA, for thy Royall Phoenix' nest.

(The Office of the Holy Crosse (Compline hymn), lines 5 - 6)

His more distant meditative stance is exemplified in the lines,

Look up, languishing Soul! Lo where the fair
BADG of thy faith calls back thy care,
    And biddes thee ne're forget
    Thy life is one long Debt
Of love to Him, who on this painfull TREE
Paid back the flesh he took for thee.

(Vexilla Regis, the Hymn of the Holy Crosse, lines 1 - 6)

As meditator, Crashaw almost invariably sets up religious icons: the bleeding crucifix, a saint such as St. Theresa or St. Mary Magdalen, the Virgin of the Assumption or the Mater Dolorosa.

Thus, although Bertonasco suggests that Crashaw neglected the Ignatian meditation,[8] the composition of place is essential to
Crashaw's poetry. But, he eschews both the soul as personification
one finds in Quarles' *Emblemes* and the interiorization inherent in
the Wiericx prints.

But the resultant distance between icon and spectator does not
totally cut Crashaw off from the use of the emblematic technique,
for he could use a peculiar combination of emblem and sensuosity
to intensify both the basic icon and the concept behind it. He expresses this specific intent when he writes about the symbolic
potentialities of the name of Jesus:

> Goe & request
> Great NATURE for the KEY of her huge Chest
> Of Heavns, the self involving Sett of Sphears
> (Which dull mortality more Feeles then heares)
> Then rouse the nest
> Of nimble ART, & traverse round
> The Aiery Shop of soul-appeasing Sound:
> And beat a summons in the Same
> All-soveraign Name
> To warn each severall kind
> And shape of sweetness.
> (*To the Name above Every Name, the Name of Jesus,* lines 28-38)

The emblematic kinds of symbols one finds in the poetry of
Donne and Herbert most certainly are evident in such images as
the key to nature's chest, the set of spheres, the nest of art, and the
shop of sound. But these images tend to melt into, and be
obscured by, the overall sensuosity of the poem. In seeking to give
both profit and pleasure to his readers, Crashaw has selected a
means of pleasing that would not have been available to the earlier
metaphysical poets. His poem on the gift of Herbert's *The Temple*
to a friend shows how far away from Herbert he could travel in
seeking to emphasize the "shape of sweetness":

> Know you faire, on what you looke;
> Divinest love lyes in this booke:
> Expecting fire from your eyes,
> To kindle this his sacrifice.
> When your hands unty these strings,
> Thinke you have an Angell by th'wings.

One that gladly will bee nigh,
To wait upon each morning sigh.
To flutter in the balmy aire,
Of your well perfumed prayer.
> *(On Mr. G. Herberts booke intitled the Temple of Sacred Poems,*
> *sent to a Gentlewoman,* lines 1 - 10)

Although the poem lauds Herbert, the emblematic qualities associated with Herbert are absent. Instead, the emphasis is on the emotional effect that Herbert's poetry will have on the reader. Crashaw's seductive angel who flutters "in the balmy aire" and waits "upon each morning sigh" suggests that the poet's orientation is one of wooing rather than, as with Herbert, one of spiritual struggle and final victory. A perusal of Quarles' *Emblemes* undoubtedly would have brought different responses from the two poets.[9] Herbert, closer in time to the Renaissance and its concept of a universe of correspondences, would have sought significant implications in the depiction of Amor's wings, while Crashaw would have emphasized their sensuous palpability.

The elements that make up that sensuosity serve to underscore Crashaw's identification with the Baroque in the visual arts: George Walton Williams has explored them under such headings as color, light and dark, quantity and liquidity.[10] These, certainly, are responsible for much of what in Crashaw's poetry reaches the emotions. But it is the combination of these sensuous qualities with the emblematic, which Bertonasco finds "at the base of Crashaw's poems,"[11] that results in the kind of visual ambiguity found in the conceit on the significance of the Magadalen's tears. When Donne and Herbert place images in seemingly incongrous combinations, we are prepared to accept the validity of those combinations because we have participated in the mental process of the meditator as he subjects them to his understanding. Crashaw, responding to the emblematic heritage but more dependent on a sensuous means of reaching us, has not worried about providing us with the logical connections between the images that constitute his pictures.[12] The following love emblem imagery with which Crashaw surrounds St. Theresa provides an excellent example:

LOVE touch't her HEART, & lo it beates
High, & burnes with such brave heates;
Such thirsts to dy, as dares drink up,

A thousand cold deaths in one cup.
> *(A Hymn to the Name and Honor of the Admirable Sainte*
> *Teresa. . . , lines 35-38)*

Here, although the heart does not represent the persona's soul and several senses are referred to, the heart is active and can behave as peculiarly as any heart in the poetry of Donne or Herbert, or in the heart emblems: it can, in effect, burn and quench its thirst by drinking from a cup. But when we have separated the action from what Crashaw is using that action to reveal we have lost much of the passage, for Crashaw so intertwines his sensuous words with the action of the poem that they cannot be effectively separated. The same is true of an emblematic image that has much in common with George Wither's print of a tongue with wings:

This foot hath got a Mouth and lippes,
  To pay the sweet summe of thy kisses:
To pay thy Teares, an Eye that weeps
  In stead of Teares such Gems as this is.
> *(On the wounds of our crucified Lord, lines 13 - 16)*

A sensuous element turned symbol can, in fact, provide the unifying element of an entire Crashaw poem.[13] In the following, the physical quality of the blood of Christ is stressed:

Jesu, no more! It is full tide.
From thy head & from thy feet,
From thy hands & from thy side
All the purple Rivers meet.
> *(Upon the Bleeding Crucifix, I)*

Those rivers ultimately become the "WELL of living WATERS," but it is through the physical element that involves such extensions as "this red sea of thy blood" and "Rain-swoln rivers" that Crashaw reaches that point. Thus, although the logic behind Crashaw's images is not always immmediately evident, the sensuous elements take on a life of their own and function in an emblematic manner. This serves to woo the reader but does not involve him intellectually in the same way as does the visual imagery of Donne and Herbert. Crashaw's images frequently do the same kinds of things that one would expect the images in an emblem print to be doing. But, unlike Donne and Herbert, who used actual images from the emblems for their own purposes, Crashaw has moved at least one step further away from the images found in existing emblem books. Donne and Herbert played with and twisted what they found in their emblematic sources; Crashaw, as Wallerstein has pointed out, is not really interested in the sources at all.[14]

Thus, the specific visual images with which Crashaw gives meaning to his central icon are the results of apparently vague and out-of-context remembrances of emblems he has seen, combined with emblematic techniques deprived of their analogical ties and brought into conformity with the growing interest in appeal to the senses that dominated the Baroque. His visual world is a strange one to the modern reader because the senuosity does not seem appropriate to the technique; but regarded within the context of his times, it takes on a logic of its own. Crashaw, although not concerned in his poetry with epistemology, has responded to the new emphasis on the senses. Stepping back to create, rather than to become involved in, the icon of his meditation, he emphasizes the growing separation between man and nature — but not between man and God — by his emphasis on sense appeal.

While Crashaw was inextricably involved in the emblem, his contemporary Vaughan was not. Vaughan could refer to the emblems of the period and use them; but he also could discard them for a more direct approach to knowledge attained through observation. For there is in Vaughan's poetry evidence of a real break with the emblematic technique. This is in accord with other observations that have been made about metaphysical poetry at mid-century. Martz, for example, notes that with Crashaw's death in 1649 "the power of liturgical and eucharistic symbols" to which the earlier poets had been oriented, "died away in English poetry"; and the appearance in 1645 of John Milton's *Poems* and in 1650 of the first edition of Vaughan's *Silex Scintillans* marked "the emergence of the layman as a central force in religious poetry of the period." The earlier poets, he writes, had in common "a devotion to the mysteries of the Passion and to a liturgy that served to celebrate those mysteries."[15] Earl Miner points out that there was a lessening of the dramatic quality in metaphysical poetry as the century progressed.[16] These are consistent with the decline in the emblematic orientation and the substitution of the visibly "real" for that which was iconographically traditional. There is, with the poetry of Vaughan, a further movement away from the emblematic heritage with which the century began.

There are, however, a number of elements in the poetry of Vaughan that would seem to relate his images to the love emblem tradition. As E.C. Pettet, in discussing the Biblical emphasis in Vaughan's poetry, has suggested, there is a relationship between Vaughan's descriptive writing and the Canticles.[17] As had Crashaw, Vaughan found inspiration in the work of Herbert. And his work bears some relationship to the seige-of-love tradition that is so evident in the work of Donne, Herbert, and Crashaw. Vaughan not only prefaced the 1650 edition of *Silex Scintillans* with a heart emblem,[18] but he also occasionally wrote in terms reminiscent of the love emblems themselves:

Sure, *holyness* the *Magnet* is,
And *Love* the *Lure,* that woos thee down;
Which makes the high transcendent bliss
Of knowing thee, so rarely known.

(The Queer, lines 13 - 16)

But there is a new emphasis in Vaughan's poetry that is inimical to the emblematic one finds in the poetry of Donne and Herbert, and even of Crashaw. Such emblematic images as hearts are less frequent in Vaughan's poetry than are more naturalistic skies and waterfalls. Although Vaughan's persona as soul often walks through allegorical landscapes, the space therein is the natural space one finds in the emblems of Quarles. Rarely do objects move out of their natural contexts and behave in unexpected ways. And, if we were to look for a counterpart to Baroque painting in Vaughan's landscapes, we would not find it in the fleshily sensuous religious works that can be associated with Crashaw's poetry but in the Dutch landscapes that already were beginning to appeal to the English affection for the countryside. For even when Vaughan writes of the heart as a "narrow, homely room" *(The dwelling-place,* line 13), he makes the reader aware that the visual context is a much larger, natural one.

Vaughan's equating of the heart or soul with a "narrow, homely room" is quite in keeping with Martz's analysis of Vaughan's poetry as representative of the Augustinian concept of interior illumination, an essentially Platonic "intuitive groping back into

regions of the soul that lie beyond sensory memories."[19] Martz
suggests a parallel between what he calls "Vaughan's characteristic
triad, the Bible, Nature, and the Self" and the emphasis by the
medieval Augustinians on the books of scripture, nature and soul
as sources of knowledge. "The three books are, essentially, one,"
writes Martz, for "the revelation given in the Bible shows man
how to read, first nature, and then his own soul."[20] Although the
ultimate goal is the book of the soul, this is not inconsistent with
the frequent observation that Vaughan insisted upon the importance of that other book, the book of nature. In this insistence lies
the major element in Vaughan's departure from the emblematic.
If, for example, we compare his poem on the last judgment with
Donne's sonnet on the same subject we can see just how far from
the emblematic concept of nature Vaughan's mind could remove
itself. Donne, of course, begins in the emblematic tradition:

At the round earths imagin'd corners, blow
Your trumpets, Angells, and arise, arise
From death, you numberlesse infinities
Of soules.

(Holy Sonnet VII, lines 1 - 4)

With the economy of the emblematist, Donne has set up his images. We can see the resulting picture very much as we can see, for
example, one of Montenay's emblems in which angels at each corner blow toward a central globe.[21] In Donne's picture, the mere
mention of the corners of the earth, the trumpets, and the angels is
expected to call forth everything that the reader has learned about
the last judgment from the Book of Revelation. The individual images can be read as an emblem would be read. Vaughan, on the
other hand, begins:

When through the North a fire shall rush
    And rowle into the East,
And like a firie torrent brush
    And sweepe up South, and West,
When all shall streame, and lighten round
    And with surprizing flames
Both stars, and Elements confound
    And quite blot out their names.

(Day of Judgement, lines 1 - 8)

Unlike Donne's picture, Vaughan's does not, of course, fit nicely into the sonnet form. It would have been difficult for Vaughan, given his orientation toward exterior nature, to have used the sonnet form in this particular instance; for Vaughan has found it necessary to present a sensuous setting for his last judgment. He has not, as Donne or an emblematist would, set forth a series of images that could, in themselves, be read; instead, he has created the scene itself. To do this Vaughan has extended his imagination in a way that neither Donne nor Herbert could have considered. He ends, as Donne does, with a colloquy; he even points out, in words reminiscent of Donne, that when the day of judgment finally arrives, it will be too late for repentance. But within the poem itself he has relaxed the metaphoric tensions that are characteristic of the poetry of either Donne or Herbert. The relaxation of those tensions has opened up new fields of exploration, both of the soul and of the exterior world. There is in Vaughan's poetry evidence that these two areas of exploration have grown much farther apart than they were in the poetry of the earlier poets. To be sure, we can find in his poetry much of the emblematic peculiarity of image. He can write, for example, of "a twin'd wreath of *grief* and *praise*" *(The Wreath,* line 9), of "a pure, and whitend soul" that "feedst among the Lillies " *(Dressing,* lines 1 - 2), or of a soul that can be hatched *(Disorder and frailty,* line 47). But this kind of configuration is not as easy to find as one might expect in the poetry of a man who had been inspired by Herbert.

Comparing Vaughan's *Regeneration* and Herbert's *The Pilgrimage,* Martz writes that in stanza four of Vaughan's poem "the Herbertian echoes fade out, as Vaughan's pilgrim is called away into an interior region of the soul" characterized by natural and Biblical images.[22] But Vaughan's utilization of the Augustinian theme of interior illumination serves to more emphatically underscore his departure from Herbertian sources and employment of imagery. Herbert's *The Pilgrimage,* which first brings the persona to a "gloomy cave of Desperation" and then to the "rock of Pride" (lines 4 - 6), presents the kind of allegorical journey one associates with John Bunyan's *The Pilgrim's Progress.* The landscape Herbert explores represents the vices; and the use of this analogy reveals a recognizable relationship to the thought-object correspondence orientation of the emblematic way of thinking. The stanza that immediately precedes the one Martz cites as an ex-

ample of Vaughan's breaking away from Herbert is as Herbertian
as anything Vaughan wrote:

So sigh'd I upwards still, at last
     'Twixt steps, and falls,
I reach'd the pinacle, where plac'd
   I found a paire of scales,
   I tooke them up and layd
     In th'one late paines,
The other smoake, and pleasures weigh'd
   But prov'd the heavier graines.

(Regeneration, lines 17 - 24)

  The poem, in fact, provides an excellent example of Vaughan's
use of the emblematic heritage in a work that is not essentially
emblematic. Although Vaughan's persona, in the above passage, is
involved in the allegorical landscape in much the same way that the
pilgrims are involved in Herbert's poem and in *The Pilgrim's Progress,* the poem contains a passage that is in direct contrast. If
ever, before James Thomson's *The Seasons,* a poem contained
lines of natural description, it is the following:

The unthrift Sunne shot vitall gold
     A thousand peeces,
And heaven its azure did unfold
   Checqur'd with snowie fleeces,
   The aire was all in spice
     And every bush
A garland wore; Thus fed my Eyes
   But all the Eare lay hush.

(Ibid., lines 41 - 48)

  However, even in the contrasting passage that contains the
emblematic scales, it is the persona himself who sighs upward and
not, as in much of the poetry of Donne and Herbert, a visualized
symbol made to act strangely. In the one passage in which the symbols do behave somewhat peculiarly, there is also a difference.
Vaughan writes of the mind as the scene of action:

   Yet, was it frost within,
     And surly winds

Blasted my infant buds, and sinne
Like Clouds ecclips'd my mind.

(Ibid., lines 5 - 8)

Within that context, although the soul becomes objectified, it becomes objectified as a natural scene depicted in contrast to the scene without. The frost-nipped buds, which may be interpreted as the thoughts of the persona, and the clouds, which may be interpreted as sin, are not visually hieroglyphic in the same sense as, for example, a tongue with wings or the picture of Christ crucified within a heart.

With the exception of the emblematic scale stanza, Vaughan's exterior landscape, which carries the burden of *Regeneration,* shows an even closer association between tenor and vehicle. For Vaughan's landscape neither exhibits hyperbolic exaggeration nor depicts objects pulled out of natural context and placed in strange relationships to one another, as does the poetry of Donne and Herbert. Grove, fountains, stones, and flowers are all part of a natural setting; his persona's body functions as one would expect a human body to function. His "Pilgrims Eye," for example,

Far from reliefe,
Measures the melancholy skye
Then drops, and rains for griefe.

(Regeneration, lines 14 - 16)

The only touch of a Herbertian or emblematic exaggeration is in the use of the word "rains." Throughout, the appeal is as much to the senses as in any poem by Crashaw; but that appeal can be relatively uncomplicated by emblematic echoes.

One of the most striking examples of Vaughan's sensuous emphasis can be seen in a comparison of the major images used by him and Herbert to express the human's soul's relation to heaven. Vaughan, as has been frequently observed, employs a natural light that is as palpable as the light imagery in *Paradise Lost.* The most frequently quoted examples are, of course, "They are all gone into the world of light!" and

I saw Eternity the other night
Like a great *Ring* of pure and endless light,
All calm, as it was bright,

And round beneath it, Time in hours, days, years,
    Driv'n by the spheres
Like a vast shadow mov'd, In which the world
    And all her train were hurl'd.

(The World, lines 1 - 8)

There are also references to, for example, "that mighty and eter-
nall light" *(Resurrection and Immortality,* line 64), to God's put-
ting on "Clouds instead of light" *(The Incarnation, and Passion,*
line 5), and to the religious light of Whitsuntide:

Welcome white day! a thousand Suns,
Though seen at once, were black to thee;
For after their light darkness comes,
But thine shines to eternity.

(White Sunday, lines 1 - 4)

    To Herbert, however, the major symbol relating the soul to
heaven is the emblematic wing that is reminiscent of the sometimes
winged figures of Amor and Anima in Quarles' *Emblemes;* and he
uses it with a frequency that almost equals Vaughan's use of light.
Herbert can "imp" his persona's wing on God's wing *(Easter-
wings,* line 19), let the soul rise and fall with the wings of music
(Church-musick, line 6) or emphasize the wings of the Holy Ghost
as dove:

Listen sweet Dove unto my song,
    And spread thy golden wings in me;
    Hatching my tender heart so long,
Till it get wing, and flie away with thee.

(Whitsunday, lines 1 - 4)

    There is a wealth of natural observation in Vaughan's poetry
that we find in that of neither Donne nor Herbert. Donne and
Herbert have truly "ransacked" nature for similitudes, but they do
not look at nature herself. They use sky, forests, and flowers as
they would any images: pictures, for example, or hearts, or any in-
animate objects. Donne's primrose and his sun serve the same
function as his windowpanes or his spheres. Herbert's "Day most
calm, most bright" becomes "the next worlds bud" *(Sunday,*
lines 1 - 2). To both, nature is something to be used wittily; the ob-

jects one finds in nature, like any others, are tools of the mind and perform their function as emblematic images. One does not feel that either Donne or Herbert walked through the natural world and responded to it as it is. It is there to be used; but its odors are not to be breathed nor its breezes felt upon the face.

Vaughan does more than merely separate the traditionally emblematic from that which can be observed through sensory experience. His persona, upon occasion, can look at visible nature, not for confirmation of what he already knows, but in order to extract a new meaning. This is quite the reverse of the emblematic method, as can be shown by a comparison of Vaughan's *The Water-fall* to a passage in which Donne also uses a stream metaphorically. Donne writes:

As streames are, Power is; those blest flowers that dwell
At the rough streames calm head, thrive and do well,
But having left their roots, and themselves given
To the streames tyrannous rage, alas, are driven
Through mills, and rockes, and woods, and at last, almost
Consum'd in going, in the sea are lost.

(Satyre III, lines 103-108)

Donne has formed an emblematic analogy between streams and power; what is true of one is therefore true of the other. Carefully working out the analogy point by point, he equates all of the characteristics of power with the characteristics of the stream. It is obvious that Donne, wanting to say something about power, selected the stream and its attributes as an appropriate vehicle. But the opposite would appear to be true of the persona in Vaughan's poem. For Vaughan's persona starts with the waterfall, sets it up as a meditative object, and then proceeds to question it:

With what deep murmurs through times silent stealth
Doth thy transparent, cool and watry wealth
   Here flowing fall,
   And chide, and call,
As if his liquid, loose Retinue staid
Lingring, and were of this steep place afraid,
   The common pass
   Where, clear as glass,
   All must descend

Not to an end:
But quickned by this deep and rocky grave,
Rise to a longer course more bright and brave.

(The Water-fall, lines 1 - 12)

This persona is not expecting a hieroglyphic message from the waterfall. Rather, he emphasizes his physical relationship with it:

Dear stream! dear bank, where often I
Have sate, and pleas'd my pensive eye.

(Ibid., lines 12 - 13)

But more important is the basis from which he *does* extract meaning from the waterfall. Having observed that the water descends to a "deep and rocky grave," but then rises "to a longer course more bright and brave," he asks:

Why, since each drop of thy quick store
Runs thither, whence it flow'd before,
Should poor souls fear a shade or night,
Who came (sure) from a sea of light?
Or since those drops are all sent back
So sure to thee, that none doth lack,
Why should frail flesh doubt any more
That what God takes, hee'l not restore?

(Ibid., lines 14 - 23)

And, because he has been able to see this relationship, he draws this conclusion:

What sublime truths, and wholesome themes,
Lodge in thy mystical, deep streams!

(Ibid., lines 27 - 28)

Although Vaughan acknowledges in the next lines that man depends upon the Holy Spirit for aid in coming to such conclusions, it is nevertheless the natural object — the waterfall itself — that provides the answer. Within the context of the poem, Vaughan has not sought to find an occult meaning in nature, but, from his observations of nature, concludes that perhaps the laws of God manifest themselves universally. Thus, although certain of Vaughan's images can be characterized as emblematic, he is also

capable of a relationship to sensory experience that is new in
metaphysical poetry. This relationship is perhaps best expressed in
his own words:

To highten thy *Devotions,* and keep low
All mutinous thoughts, what business e'r thou hast
Observe God in his works; here *fountains* flow,
Birds sing, *Beasts* feed, *Fish* leap, and th'*Earth* stands fast;
    Above are restless *motions,* running *Lights,*
    Vast Circling *Azure,* giddy *Clouds,* days, nights.

When *Seasons* change, then lay before thine Eys
His wondrous *Method;* mark the various *Scenes*
In heav'n; *Hail, Thunder, Rain-bows, Snow,* and *Ice,*
Calmes, Tempests, Light, and *darkness* by his means;
    Thou canst not misse his Praise; Each *tree, herb, flowre*
    Are shadows of his *wisedome,* and his Pow'r.
                  (*Rules and Lessons*, lines 85-96)

    It is just such passages that suggest comparison with the poetry
of Traherne, whose work was first thought to be that of
Vaughan.[23] Of all the seventeenth-century religious poets to whom
custom has accorded the designation "metaphysical," Traherne
has left poems that seem the most difficult to classify. The stylistic
characteristics that the others share, to one degree or another, are
conspicuously absent in Traherne's poetry. While Traherne, more
than any other metaphysical poet, proclaims the validity of
knowledge obtained through the senses, the eye that Traherne so
joyfully celebrates does not encumber the mind of poet or reader
with either traditional hieroglyph or the minutiae of visual observation. In fact, he told his potential readers that he would use no
"curling Metaphors that gild the Sence" but would present instead, "real Crowns and Thrones and Diadems!" *(The Author to
the Critical Peruser,* line 11). To him, those who adorn poetry with
clothes and coverings overlook man's body and mind, which are
God's works, and instead magnify their own works. It is man in
terms of the senses that is important to Traherne. For, it is because
of what the senses allow man to perceive about God that he lauds
them:

My Senses were Informers to my Heart,
The Conduits of his Glory Power and Art.

His Greatness Wisdom Goodness I did see,
His Glorious Lov, and his Eternitie,
Almost as soon as Born: and evry Sence
Was in me like to som Intelligence.

(Nature, lines 7 - 13)

Thus he criticizes those who would obscure the truth that man can
discover through his senses:

Ev'n thus do idle Francies, Toys and Words,
(Like Gilded Scabbards hiding rusty Swords)
Take vulgar Souls; who gaze on rich Attire
But God's diviner Works do ne're admire.

(The Author to the Critical Peruser, lines 61 - 64)

But, as A. L. Clements points out, Traherne did not mean to ex-
clude metaphor from his poetry any more than did Herbert.[24] His
emphasis is on the visually true; and he strips his poetry of all he
feels would complicate that truth:

The Naked Things
Are most Sublime, and Brightest shew,
    When they alone are seen:
    Mens Hands then Angels Wings
Are truer Wealth even here below:
    For those but seem.
Their Worth they then do best reveal,
When we all Metaphores remove,
    For Metaphores conceal,
    And only Vapours prove.

(The Person, lines 17 - 26)

In fact, in the last line of the above passage, as Clements points
out, it is precisely a metaphor he uses to emphasize his denial of
metaphors. But, in the lines that follow, he treats the human
body's relationship to the universe in a way quite different from
that of Donne or Herbert:

They best are Blazond when we see
    The Anatomie,
Survey the Skin, cut up the Flesh, the Veins
Unfold: The Glory there remains.

The Muscles, Fibres, Arteries and Bones
Are better far then Crowns and precious Stones.

(Ibid., lines 27 - 32)

We find here no "little world made cunningly" of, for example, arteries that Renaissance writers could compare to rivers. Instead, the common Renaissance metaphor of correspondence has been discarded in favor of a celebration of the body for itself. As an instrument of sense, the body is no longer a microcosmic reflection of the macrocosm nor a cage wherein the soul is imprisoned until death releases it; it has, in fact, been glorified as a valuable means of revealing truths about God. Traherne's relation to metaphor, therefore, is a nebulous one. As Clements shows, there are basic, overall metaphors, such as that of childhood used to represent the redeemed state,[25] which run throughout Traherne's poetry. But a look at specific metaphors within individual poems shows that Traherne's metaphors are considerably different from the conceits of the other metaphysical poets.

Traherne, most certainly, can speak of Truth as the daughter of Eternity and as his persona's bride *(The Designe,* lines 46 - 54), of the "Worlds fair Beauty" setting his persona's soul on fire *(Nature,* line 6), or of his persona as an ocean *(Silence,* line 70). But not only does he not insist on pointing out logical connections between tenor and vehicle, he also does not bring these to actual visualization. We can see how much he differs from the other metaphysical poets if we examine the context of his ocean metaphor. Here Traherne writes of the relationship of the persona, the visible world, and God:

His Gifts, and my Possessions, both our Treasures;
He mine, and I the Ocean of his Pleasures.
He was an Ocean of Delights from Whom
The Living Springs and Golden Streams did com:
My Bosom was an Ocean into which
They all did run. And me they did enrich.
A vast and Infinit Capacitie,
Did make my Bosom like the Deitie,
In Whose Mysterious and Celestial Mind
All Ages and all Worlds together shind.
Who tho he nothing said did always reign,
And in Himself Eternitie contain.

The world was more in me, then I in it.
The King of Glory in my Soul did sit.

(Ibid., lines 69 - 82)

This passage is, of course, a poetic expression of the process whereby, as Richard Douglas Jordan has shown in relation to the *Centuries,* the empty soul of innate capacity fills itself with knowledge of eternity and of God. It also suggests what has been shown in the images of Donne and Herbert to be some of the elements of the interiorized image. A bosom into which an ocean can pour and a king sitting in a soul would seem at first to be related to the interiors of hearts on which the souls of the persona in Donne's and Herbert's poetry act out their struggles as on a stage. But Traherne does not carry his imagery to actual visualization as did the earlier poets. For, while the words "ocean" and "bosom" represent concrete entities capable of visualization, Traherne does nothing here to make the reader actually see them. Furthermore, the reader is not shown, within the context of this particular metaphor, the form or category of the "Delights" that make up the ocean; nor is he given the means whereby he can visualize the soul. Thus Traherne does not really present us with a picture; instead he indiscriminately combines abstract nouns with nouns that could lead to visualization if their potentialities were carried out. But he does not find it necessary to puruse those potentialities.

Clements has shown that Traherne presents us with essentially two kinds of images. One is a catalogue or listing of objects:[26]

Properties themselves were mine,
      And Hedges Ornaments;
Walls, Boxes, Coffers, and their rich Contents
   Did not Divide my Joys, but shine.

(Wonder, lines 57 - 60)

The other is the repetitive use of objects which, partly because of their frequent repetition, take on the significance of mystical symbols. The most frequently repeated, Clements finds, are "Eye," "Sphere," "Sun," "Mirror," "King," "Dwelling Place," and "Fountain"; and less frequently repeated are such words as "abyss," "angel," "bride," "friend," and "vine".[27] But with the exception of the addition of adjectives, such as adjectives of color, these nouns stand for themselves in the immediate context; and, in the overall context, they stand as representatives of the world of knowledge with which the soul is ultimately filled as it exercises its capacity for achieving eternity. The process is cumulative and intuitive; it is not intellectual. Thus Traherne does not involve himself in the metaphoric intricacies that characterize metaphysical poetry in general. There are no hidden or occult meanings or remnants of such; and tenor and vehicle are so close together that Clements finds Traherne's unadorned style may be "looking forward to the next literary period, with its Johnsonian censuring of the hyperbolic conceit."[28]

What is immediately apparent as a major difference between the imagery used by Traherne and that used by the other meditative poets is that Traherne's poetry contains none of those elements that would classify an image as emblematic. In none of his images is the reader required to visualize and then draw intellectual conclusions from that visualization. The remnants of the hieroglyphically occult that characterize the poetry of Donne and Herbert and that were consistent with their skepticism regarding the validity of sense experience have given way to something more akin to the wonder in nature itself. This wonderment is expressed in the next century by Anthony Ashley Cooper, third Earl of Shaftesbury:

O glorious nature! supremely fair and sovereignly good! all-loving and all lovely, all divine! whose looks are so becoming and of such infinite grace; whose study brings such wisdom, and whose contemplation such delight; whose every single work affords an ampler scene, and is a nobler spectacle than all which ever art presented![29]

Traherne, of course, had to work out his own epistemological theory and incorporate it into his poetry in order to arrive at a dependence on the senses that, through John Locke's *An Essay Concerning Humane Understanding,* would become the accepted epistemological approach by the time Shaftesbury made his exuberant statement. But with Traherne, the tie with the medieval concept of a universe of correspondences and its effect on visual imagery has been definitely broken. For, although Donne and Herbert had twisted the images they used around in their minds until these images became something quite original, the basic images themselves were those that had become visual only through their use in the traditions of the past. They were, for the most part, images whose meanings were not inherent in nature itself and were literary in the sense that they had attained significance through long usage. If one did not have reference to the epistemological changes that were occurring in the seventeenth century, it would seem almost paradoxical that Crashaw should emphasize the senses, that Vaughan should draw fresh images from the physical world, and that Traherne should laud sensory experience itself. This is not to say, however, that any of the metaphysical poets, even Traherne, had in any way achieved a Lockean position in regard to epistemology. Rather they responded to the episemological upheaval that, because of the seventeenth-century's growing emphasis on scientific observation, was a part of the *Zeitgeist*.

NOTES

Chapter I

1. Mary Paton Ramsay, one of the first critics to attempt to place Donne's work in philosophical context, found that Donne's style was natural to a poet schooled in the theology of the middle ages; see *Les Doctrines médiévales chez Donne*, 2nd ed. (London: Oxford Univ. Press, 1924), p. 266, *et passim*. That Donne was bound by medieval philosophy was challenged in 1936 by Charles Monroe Coffin; see *John Donne and the New Philosophy*, 2nd ed. (New York: Humanities Press, 1958). However, more recent critics often tend to agree with Ramsay.

2. "Sermon No. 9," *The Sermons of John Donne,* ed. E.M. Simpson and G.R. Potter, 10 vols. (Berkeley: Univ. of California Press, 1953-1962), VIII, p. 221.

3. I Cor. XIII. 12.

4. Quotation of Donne's poetry is from *The Poems of John Donne,* ed. H.J.C. Grierson, 2 vols. (London: Oxford Univ. Press, 1912), I. Throughout my text, I have modernized all typographical variations.

5. Quotation of Traherne's poetry is from *Thomas Traherne: Centuries, Poems, and Thanksgivings,* ed. H.M. Margoliouth, 2 vols. (Oxford: Clarendon Press, 1958), II. Where Margoliouth has included versions from both the Dobell Folio and *Poems of Felicity,* I have cited the Dobell version.

6. K.G. Hamilton, *The Two Harmonies: Poetry and Prose in the Seventeenth Century* (Oxford: Clarendon Press, 1963), p. 177.

7. Quotation of Davies' poetry is from *The Poems of Sir John Davies,* ed. R.

Krueger (Oxford: Clarendon Press, 1975).

8. E.M.W. Tillyard, *The Elizabethan World Picture*, (London: Chatto and Windus, 1943), pp. 1 - 6.

9. For a discussion of the influence of Lockean epistemology on eighteenth-century English poetry see Kenneth MacLean, *John Locke and English Literature of the Eighteenth Century* (New York: Russell, 1962), pp. 49 - 102.

10. Roy Daniells, *Milton, Mannerism and Baroque* (Toronto: Univ. of Toronto Press, 1963), pp. 11 - 12.

11. Coffin has shown that Donne selected imagery representative of conflicting philosophies and theories to suit his own poetic purposes. See *John Donne and the New Philosophy, passim.*

12. Frank Manley, ed., *John Donne: The Anniversaries* (Baltimore: Johns Hopkins Press, 1963), p. 18.

13. *Ibid.,* pp. 19 - 50.

14. Hiram Haydn, *The Counter Renaissance* (New York: Scribner's, 1950), p. 160.

15. See Marjorie Hope Nicolson, *The Breaking of the Circle: Studies in the Effect of the "New Science" upon Seventeenth-Century Poetry,* 2nd ed., rev. (New York: Columbia Univ. Press, 1960), p. 82. Nicolson regards *The Anniversaries* as "companion poems" that achieve "harmony" out of "cacophony."

16. R.L. Colie, "The Rhetoric of Transcendence," *Philological Quarterly,* 43 (1964), 161. For other discussions of Donne's skepticism see Bredvold, "The Naturalism of Donne in Relation to Some Renaissance Traditions," *Journal of English and Germanic Philology,* 22 (1923), 471-502, and "The Religious Thought of Donne in Relation to Medieval and Later Traditions," *Studies in Shakespeare, Milton, and Donne,* University of Michigan Publications in Language and Literature, I (New York: MacMillan, 1925), 193-232; Robert Ornstein, "Donne, Montaigne and Natural Law," *Journal of English and Germanic Philology,* 55 (1956), 213-299; and George Williamson, "The Libertine Donne," *Philological Quarterly,* 13 (1934), 276-291.

17. Coffin, *John Donne and the New Philosophy,* p. 20.

18. Colie, "The Rhetoric of Transcendence," 161.

19. Victor Harris, *All Coherence Gone* (Chicago: Univ. of Chicago Press, 1959) pp. 143-167.

20. Haydn, *The Counter Renaissance,* p. 164.

21. Erwin Panofsky, *Idea, a Concept in Art Theory,* trans. J.S. Peake, 2nd ed. (Columbia, S.C.: Univ. of South Carolina Press, 1968), p. 5.

22. Although Donne goes on to say that the virtuous man still remains, he nevertheless claims that he cannot name the specific virtues.

23. For a concise exposition of this emphasis, see Forrest G. Robinson, *The*

Shape of Things Known: Sidney's "Apology" in Its Philosophical Traditions (Cambridge, Mass.: Harvard Univ. Press, 1972), pp. 11 - 59.

24. Helen Gardner, ed., *John Donne, The Divine Poems* (Oxford: Clarendon Press, 1952), p. xxxi.

25. Quotation of Herbert's poetry is from *The Works of George Herbert,* ed. F.E. Hutchinson (Oxford: Clarendon Press, 1945).

26. Laurence Howard Jacobs, "Knowledge in the Poetry of George Herbert," Diss. Univ. of California, Berkeley, 1970, p. 82.

27. *Ibid.,* p. 58.

28. *Ibid.,* p. 57.

29. *Ibid.,* pp. 26-27.

30. *Ibid.,* pp. 60-61.

31. Quotation of Crashaw's poetry is from *The Poems English Latin and Greek of Richard Crashaw,* ed. L.C. Martin, 2nd ed. (Oxford: Clarendon Press, 1957).

32. Quotation of Vaughan's poetry is from *The Works of Henry Vaughan,* ed. L.C. Martin, 2nd ed. (Oxford: Clarendon Press, 1957).

33. See Louis L. Martz, *The Poetry of Meditation: A Study in English Religious Literature of the Seventeenth Century,* 2nd ed. (New Haven: Yale Univ. Press, 1962), pp. 150-152. Although Vaughan's poetry frequently has been associated with the Hermetic tradition, Martz writes that the imagery in *Vanity of Spirit* "reminds us that the fundamental inspiration for Vaughan's finest achievements does not lie in the occult but in the great, central meditative tradition."

34. Thomas Traherne, *Centuries, Poems and Thanksgivings,* II, p. 3.

35. John Locke, *An Essay Concerning Human Understanding,* ed. A. C. Fraser, 2 vols. (New York: Dover Publications, 1959), I, p. 99.

36. See Carol L. Marks, "Thomas Traherne and Cambridge Platonism," *PMLA,* 81 (1966), 521-534. Marks stresses affinity, not derivation.

37. Nicolson, *The Breaking of the Circle,* p. 168.

38. Toshihiko Kawasaki, "Donne's Microcosm," *Seventeenth-Century Imagery: Essays on Uses of Figurative Language from Donne to Farquhar,* ed. E. Miner (Berkeley: Univ. of California Press, 1971), p. 28.

39. John Donne, *Devotions Upon Emergent Occasions,* ed. A. Raspa (Montreal: McGill-Queens Univ. Press, 1975), pp. 19-20.

40. Nicolson, *The Breaking of the Circle,* pp. 196-201.

41. Donne, *Devotions Upon Emergent Occasions,* p. 20.

42. Stanley Stewart, *The Expanded Voice: The Art of Thomas Traherne* (San Marino, Calif.: Huntington Library, 1970), *passim.*

43.Richard Douglas Jordan, *The Temple of Eternity: Thomas Traherne's Philosophy of Time* (Port Washington: Kennikat Press, 1972), p. 99.

44.*Ibid.,* p. 57.

45.*Ibid.,* p. 45.

46.*Ibid.,* pp. 18 - 28

47.*Ibid.,* p. 18. Jordan quotes, for example, Traherne's reference in the *Centuries* (II, 51) to physical existence as "a Dull Lump of Heavy Clay, by which thou art retarded, rather than doest move."

48.Mario Praz, *Studies in Seventeenth-Century Imagery,* 2nd ed. (Rome: Edizioni di Storia e Letteratura, 1964), pp. 14 - 16.

49.Joseph A. Mazzeo, "Metaphysical Poetry, and the Poetry of Correspondence," (rev. "Metaphysical Poetry and the Poetic of Correspondence, *JHI,* 14 (1953), *Renaissance and Seventeenth-Century Studies* (New York: Columbia Univ. Press, and London: Routledge, 1964) pp. 54-58. Although he does not pursue the point, Marc F. Bertonasco suggests, in reference to Crashaw, that symbols "no longer enjoyed a secure place in a grand, perfectly coherent allegorical scheme" and that the fragmentation probably was necessary if symbols were to be used for either contemplation or psychological analysis. See *Crashaw and the Baroque* (University, Ala.: Univ. of Alabama Press, 1971), p. 24.

Chapter II

1. Praz, *Studies in Seventeenth-Century Imagery,* p. 15.

2. Martz, *The Poetry of Meditation,* pp. 5 - 13.

3. Gordon S. Haight, "The Sources of Quarles *Emblemes,*" *The Library,* 4th series, 16 (1935), 189. Haight found that the prints in books I and II were copies from *Typus Mundi* (Antwerp, 1627), produced by the College of Rhetoric of the Society of Jesus of Antwerp, and that the prints in books III and IV were copied from Herman Hugo's *Pia Desideria* (Antwerp, 1624).

4. *Ibid.,* p. 188; twelve editions of the *Emblemes* were printed before 1700.

5. See Eleanor James ("The Emblem as an Image-pattern in Some Metaphysical Poetry," Diss. Univ. of Wisconsin, 1942, pp. 270-275), who points out a similarity between a number of Herbert's images and the prints in Hugo's *Pia Desideria.* See also Mary Cole Sloane, "Emblem and Meditation: Some Parallels in John Donne's Imagery," *South Atlantic Bulletin,* 39 (May, 1974), 74 - 79.

6. Martz, *The Poetry of Meditation,* p. 38.

7. *Ibid.,* pp. 27 - 28.

8. *Ibid.,*p. 31.

9. Rosemary Freeman, *English Emblem Books* (1948: rpt. New York: Octagon

Books, 1966), pp. 168-169. The significance of the titles to Herbert's poetry is discussed also by Mary Ellen Rickey, although she does not emphasize the visual; see *Utmost Art: Complexity in the Verse of George Herbert* (Lexington, Ky.: Univ. of Kentucky Press, 1966), pp. 92-102.

10. Liselotte Dieckmann, "Renaissance Hieroglyphics," *Comparative Literature,* 9 (1957), 312-318. The relationship between Dürer's woodcut and the emblem has been noted by Ludwig Volkmann, *Bilderschriften der Renaissance, Hieroglyphic und Emblematic in Ihren Beziehungen und Fortwirkungen,* 2nd ed. (Nieuwkoop: B. de Graaf, 1923), pp. 87 - 88.

11. Martz, *The Poetry of Meditation,* p. 54.

12. Francis Quarles, *Emblemes,* (London, 1635), p. 96.

13. *Ibid.,* p. 12.

14. James ("The Emblem as an Image-pattern in Some Metaphysical Poetry," p. 117) pointed out that Donne used the emblem "as a method of analysis which approximates the emblem verse."

15. Rosemond Tuve, *A Reading of George Herbert* (Chicago: Univ. of Chicago Press, 1952), pp. 103 - 105.

16. Tuve, *Elizabethan and Metaphysical Imagery,* 2nd ed. (Chicago: Univ. of Chicago Press, 1961), p. 53.

17. Joan Evans, *Pattern: A Study of Ornament in Western Europe from 1180-1900,* 2 vols. (Oxford: Clarendon Press, 1931), I, pp. 156 - 159.

18. Georgette de Montenay, *Emblemes, ou devises chrestiennes* (Lyons, 1571), p. 4.

19. The lost ship image of the Petrarchan sonnets found its way into religious emblems relatively early; Montenay *(Ibid.,* p. 11) had used it to indicate that only God can guide man safely through life. There are two such depictions in Quarles' *Emblemes.* In one (p. 164), Anima, struggling in a stormy sea, reaches toward a welcoming Amor, who waits on a rocky shore. In the other, (p. 232), Amor carries Anima to safety while others struggle in the sea.

20. In Quarles' *Emblemes,* for example, the eye of God peers out of the clouds at Anima, who holds the world in her hand, and at Amor, who holds a heart (p. 120); Book III is prefaced by an emblem that depicts the eye and ears of God in the clouds (p. 124). See also Montenay, *Emblems, ou devises chrestiennes,* pp. 4, 10, 11, 13.

21. Freeman, *English Emblem Books,* pp. 18 - 19.

22. Tillyard, "Foreward," *English Emblem Books,* p. viii.

23. Volkmann *(Bilderschriften der Renaissance,* p. 2) acknowledged the medieval roots of the emblem when he found the emblem to be composed of symbolism from the middle ages, the classics, and the Bible.

24. See Sears Jayne, "Ficino and the Platonism of the English Renaissance," *Comparative Literature,* 4 (1952), 214 - 218.

25. E.H. Gombrich, *"Icones Symbolicae,* the Visual Image in Neo-Platonic Thought," *Journal of the Warburg and Courtauld Institutes,* 11 (1948), 180. He points out that the sixteenth-century mind did not always make the distinction between man-made symbols and supernatural omens.

26. Dieckmann, "Renaissance Hieroglyphics," 307.

27. George Boas, ed., *The Hieroglyphics of Horapollo,* trans. Boas, Bollingen Series XXIII (Princeton: Princeton Univ. Press, 1950), p.28.

28. *The Hieroglyphics of Horapollo,* p. 84.

29. George Wither, *A Collection of Emblemes, Ancient and Moderne* (London, 1635), p. 139.

30. Tuve, *A Reading of George Herbert,* p. 153.

31. *The Hieroglyphics of Horapollo,* p. 57.

32. Henry Peacham, *Minerva Britanna* (London, 1612), p. 40.

33. Wither, *A Collection of Emblemes,* p. 48.

34. Geffrey Whitney, *A Choice of Emblemes,* ed. H. Green (1866; rpt. New York: Benjamin Blom, 1967), p. 205.

35. Thomas O. Sloan, "The Rhetoric of the Poetry of John Donne," *Studies in English Literature, 1500 - 1900,* 3 (1963), 34 - 36. Earl Miner, *The Metaphysical Mode from Donne to Cowley* (Princeton: Princeton Univ. Press, 1969, p. 133 ff) finds that the dialectic in metaphysical poetry is distinguished by its motion.

36. Sloan, "The Rhetoric of the Poetry of John Donne," 42.

37. Panofsky, *Studies in Iconology: Humanistic Themes in the Art of the Renaissance,* 2nd ed. (New York: Harper, 1962), pp. 110 - 112.

38. *Ibid.,* p. 102. Panofsky points out that Ovid's two arrows multiplied into many during the middle ages and frequently were divided into unfavorable leaden and favorable golden ones.

39. C.S. Lewis, *Studies in Medieval and Renaissance Literature* (Cambridge: Cambridge Univ. Press, 1966), p. 166.

40. Josef Lederer, "John Donne and the Emblematic Practice," *Review of English Studies,* 22 (1946), 194.

41. Donald L. Guss, *John Donne, Petrarchist: Intalianate Conceits and Love Theory in "The Songs and Sonets"* (Detroit: Wayne State Univ. Press, 1966), p. 158.

42. Praz, *Studies in Seventeenth-Century Imagery,* p. 13.

43. James, "The Emblem as Image-pattern in Some Metaphysical Poetry," p. 35.

44. *Ibid.*

45. Otho Vaenius, *Amorum Emblemata* (Antwerp, 1608), pp. 102 - 103.

46. Wither, *A Collection of Emblemes,* p. 40.

47. Whitney, *A Choice of Emblemes,* p. 219.

48. Antwerp, 1565. Cited by Green in Whitney, *A Choice of Emblemes,* p. 251.

49. Paris, 1540; Lyons, 1562. Cited *Ibid.,* pp. 329, 341.

50. Wither, "To the Majestie of Great Britain, France, and Ireland . . ." *A Collection of Emblemes,* n.p.

51. *Ibid.,* p. 111.

52. Sir Francis Bacon, *Advancement of Learning* V, v, in *The Works of Francis Bacon,* eds. J. Spedding, R. Ellis, and P. Heath, 15 vols. (1857 - 1874; rpt. New York: Garrett Press, 1968), IV, p. 537.

53. Quarles, *Emblemes,* "To the Reader," n.p. In spite of the fact that he could write of the hieroglyphics of God and although he used actual emblems as the basis of his verse, Quarles, for the most part, did not write verses that were in themselves emblematic.

54. Sir Thomas Browne, "Religio Medici," *Works of Sir Thomas Browne,* ed. C. Sayle, 3 vols. (Edinburgh: Grant, 1912), I, p. 86.

55. Tuve, *Elizabethan and Metaphysical Imagery,* p. 264.

56. Freeman, *English Emblem Books,* pp. 115 - 121.

57. Tuve, *A Reading of George Herbert,* pp. 79 - 80.

58. Such combinations, which appeared frequently in the emblem books, usually were accompanied by the motto, *festine lente.*

59. Matt. X. 16.

60. See Guss, *John Donne, Petrarchist,* pp. 61 - 80.

61. Quarles, *Emblemes,* p. 232.

62. *The Hieroglyphics of Horapollo,* p. 104.

63. Vaenius, *Amorum Emblemata,* pp. 56 - 57.

64. Praz, *Studies in Seventeenth-Century Imagery,* p. 15.

Chapter III

1. James B. Leishman, *The Monarch of Wit,* 3rd ed. (London: Hutchinson, 1957), pp. 205 - 206.

2. Miner, *The Metaphysical Mode from Donne to Cowley,* pp. 3 - 4. See also pp. 15-23.

3. *Ibid.,* pp. 4 - 5.

4. Morris W. Croll, "The Baroque Style in Prose," *Studies in English Philology: A Miscellany in Honor of Frederick Klaeber,* eds. K. Malone and M.B. Ruud (Minneapolis: Univ. of Minnesota Press, 1929), p. 271.

5. D.H. Roberts, "Just such disparitie: The Real and the Representation in

Donne's Poetry," *South Atlantic Bulletin,* 41 (Nov., 1976), 99. See also Mary Cole Sloane, "Image as Emblem in John Donne's Poetry," Diss. Univ. of Miami, 1971, pp. 115 - 120.

6. Freeman, *English Emblem Books,* pp. 119 - 120.

7. Quarles, *Emblemes,* p. 264.

8. In regard to the meditation, this was emphasized by Martz who, like Freeman, indicated that emblem and meditation were related. See Freeman, *English Emblem Books,* p. 174, and Martz, *The Poetry of Meditation,* p. 61, n. 4.

9. Quarles, *Emblemes,* p. 125. The print, p. 124, sets the theme of book III by depicting a figure shot in the breast with a dart. *Pia Desideria* is more strongly based on the Canticles than is *Typus Mundi.*

10. Praz, *Studies in Seventeenth-Century Imagery,* p. 135.

11. Robert Southwell, epistle prefatory to *Saint Peters Complaint,* 1595 (Quoted by Martz in *The Poetry of Meditation,* p. 179).

12. "Sermon No. 5," *Sermons,* I, p. 237.

13. Montenay, *Emblemes, ou devises chrestiennes,* p. 1.

14. "A tres illustre et vertueuse princesse . . .," *Ibid.,* n.p.

15. Quarles, *Emblemes,* p. 188.

16. *Ibid.,* p. 168.

17. Martz, *The Poem of the Mind* (New York: Oxford Univ. Press, 1966), p. 5. See also Mary Cole Sloane, "Emblem and Meditation: Some Parallels in John Donne's Poetry," *South Atlantic Bulletin,* 39 (May, 1974), pp. 74 - 79.

18. Quarles, *Emblemes,* p. 192.

19. *Ibid.,* p. 160.

20. *Ibid.,* p. 172.

21. Freeman noted a relationship between the emblematic Amor and Anima and *Love III.* See *English Emblem Books,* p. 164.

22. Quarles, *Emblemes,* p. 160.

23. Freeman, *English Emblem Books,* p. 120.

24. Montenay *(Emblemes, ou devises chrestiennes,* p. 4), for example, shows a skeleton trying to draw a man toward him by a rope around the neck; the hand of God holds a magnet to draw the man toward heaven. Wither *(A Collection of Emblemes,* p. 1) uses a print depicting a man contemplating a globe while death as skeleton holds a scepter and contemplates a crown and jewels.

25. Freeman, *English Emblem Books,* p. 164. She also noted the relationship of *Good Friday* to the cardiomorphic emblem tradition.

26. Karl J. Höltgen, "Ein Emblemfolge in Donne's *Holy Sonnet XIV,*" *Archiv für das studium der neueren Sprachen und Literaturen,* 200 (1963), 347 - 352.

27.Montenay, *Emblemes, ou devises chrestiennes,* p. 5.

28.*Ibid.,* p. 25.

29.Daniel Cramer, *Emblemata Sacra* (1624), p. 17. James "The Emblem as Image-Pattern in Some Metaphysical Poetry," pp. 268 - 269) pointed out that there was a relationship between some of Herbert's imagery and Cramer's emblem book, as well as other emblem books in the cardiomorphic tradition.

30.Cramer, *Emblemata Sacra,* pp. 103, 177, 77, 49, 183, 201, 37, 20.

31.Benedictus van Haeften, *Scola Cordis,* 1629.

32.Francesco Pona, *Cardiomorphoseos,* 1645.

33.Haeften, *Regia Via Crucis,* 1635.

34.Höltgen, "Ein Emblemfolge in Donne's *Holy Sonnet XIV,*" 347.

35.Quarles, *Emblemes,* p. 168.

36.Haeften, *Scola Cordis,* p. 196.

37.*The Literature of Medieval England,* ed. D.W. Robertson (New York: McGraw Hill, 1970), p. 36. The comparison was suggested by Mara Johnson in "In Search of the Divine," (unpublished paper, Florida Atlantic University, 1975), p. 8.

38.Antonius Wiericx, *Cor Jesu Amanti Sacrum* (Folger copy, ca. 1620).

39.Martz, *The Poem of the Mind,* p. 76.

40.Wiericx, *Cor Jesu Amanti Sacrum.*

41.Lederer, "John Donne and the Emblematic Practice," p. 182.

42.See Praz, *Studies in Seventeenth-Century Imagery,* p. 44.

43.Quarles, *Emblemes,* p. 152. The Biblical quotation referred to is Jeremiah IX. 1.

44.Phineas Fletcher, *The Purple Island, or the Isle of Man,* 1633.

45.Nicolson, *The Breaking of the Circle,* pp. 132 - 133.

46.Peacham, *Minerva Britanna,* p. 142.

47.Montenay, *Emblemes, ou devises chrestiennes,* p. 52.

48.Wither, *A Collection of Emblemes,* p. 42.

Chapter IV

1. Ruth C. Wallerstein, *Richard Crashaw; A Study in Style and Poetic Development,* 2nd ed. (Madison: Univ. of Wisconsin Press, 1962), pp. 10 - 13, *passim.*

2. *The Poems English Latin and Greek of Richard Crashaw,* p. 235.

3. Praz, *Studies in Seventeenth-Century Imagery,* p. 118.

4. Austin Warren, *Richard Crashaw; A Study in Baroque Sensibility,* 2nd ed. (Ann Arbor, Mich.: Univ. of Michigan Press, 1957), pp. 63 - 76.

5. Bertonasco, *Crashaw and the Baroque,* p. 28.

6. Wallerstein *(Richard Crashaw,* p. 51) indicated that there was a relationship between Crashaw's poetry and the Canticles. Bertonasco *(Crashaw and the Baroque,* pp. 28 - 39) points to several parallels between Crashaw's imagery and the prints used by Quarles for his *Emblemes.* The underlying influence of the Canticles on Crashaw's poetry frequently has been mentioned.

7. Bertonasco, *Crashaw and the Baroque,* p. 67.

8. Bertonasco *(Crashaw and the Baroque,* pp. 82 - 83) points out that actual visualization, which would correspond to the Ignatian composition of place, was optional in the Salesian meditation.

9. Both Bertonasco *(Ibid.,* pp. 32 - 37) and Wallerstein *(Richard Crashaw,* pp. 114 - 115) suggest a relationship between the prints Quarles used and some of Crashaw's imagery.

10. George Walton Williams has made a detailed exploration of various aspects of Crashaw's sensuosity. See *Image and Symbol in the Sacred Poetry of Richard Crashaw* (Columbia, S.C.: Univ. of South Carolina Press, 1963).

11. Bertonasco, *Crashaw and the Baroque,* p. 6.

12. The difference between Crashaw and Donne, in this respect, has been noted frequently; see, for example, Bertonasco, *Crashaw and the Baroque,* p. 38.

13. See Bertonasco, *Crashaw and the Baroque,* pp. 114 - 116.

14. The personal element in many of Crashaw's symbols was emphasized by Wallerstein, who regarded Crashaw's relation to the emblem, and other sources of influence, as "a kind of intellectual discipline akin in the artistic realm to the discipline in the religious realm, of mastering the technique of meditation." See *Richard Crashaw,* pp. 86, 135.

15. Martz, *The Paradise Within: Studies in Vaughan, Traherne and Milton* (New Haven: Yale Univ. Press, 1964), pp. 3 - 4.

16. See Miner, *The Metaphysical Mode from Donne to Cowley,* pp. 97 - 117. Miner sees Crashaw's poetry as exhibiting the beginning in the decline of dramatic emphasis.

17. E.C. Pettet, *Of Paradise and Light: A Study of Vaughan's "Silex Scintillans"* (Cambridge : Cambridge Univ. Press, 1960), p. 33.

18. *The Works of Henry Vaughan,* pp. 386 - 387. Vaughan, however, did not use the emblem in the 1655 edition; see Martz, *The Paradise Within,* p. 5.

19. Martz, *The Paradise Within,* p. 23.

20. *Ibid.,* p. 17.

21. Montenay, *Emblemes, ou devises chrestiennes,* p. 6.

22.Martz, *The Paradise Within,* p. 9.

23.See Gladys I. Wade, *Thomas Traherne* (1944; rpt. New York: Octagon Books, 1969), pp. 7 - 10.

24.A.L. Clements, *The Mystical Poetry of Thomas Traherne,* (Cambridge, Mass.: Harvard Univ. Press, 1969), pp. 37 - 38.

25.*Ibid.,* p. 18.

26.*Ibid.,* p. 40.

27.*Ibid.,* p. 44.

28.*Ibid.,* p. 38.

29.Anthony Ashley Cooper, third Earl of Shaftesbury, *Characteristics of Men, Manners, Opinions, Times,* ed. J.M. Robertson, 2nd ed. (Indianapolis: Bobbs-Merrill, 1964), p. 327.

1 ABOVE: Goergette de Montenay,
Emblemes ou devises chrestiennes, 1571.
By permission of the British Library.

RIGHT: Francis Quarles, *Emblemes,* 1635.
by permission of the Folger Shakespeare Library.

3 RIGHT: Antonius Wiericx,
(Cor Jesu Amanti Sacrum). ca. 1620.
By permission of the Folger Shakespeare Library.

4 BELOW: Daniel Cramer, *Emblemata Sacra,* 1624.
By permission of the British Library.

5 ABOVE: George Wither,
A Collection of Emblemes, 1635.
By permission of the British Library.

6 RIGHT: Francis Quarles, *Emblemes*, 1635.
By permission of the Folger Shakespeare Library.